Mexican Americans

Mexican Americans

by Alexandra Bandon

New York

Maxwell Macmillan Canada
Toronto

Maxwell Macmillan International
New York   Oxford   Singapore   Sydney

ACKNOWLEDGMENT

*Special thanks to the immigrants who shared their personal stories.
Their names have been change to protect their privacy.*

PHOTO CREDITS
Front cover: George Rodriguez
Front and back cover (flag photo): Richard Bachmann
UPI/Bettmann: 9, 12, 28, 56
George Rodriguez: 15, 24, 27, 34, 44, 53, 62, 65, 68, 71, 80, 83, 88, 91, 94, 100-101
Ken Light (©1988 Ken Light): 16, 30, 39, 47, 76
Richard Bachmann: 105

New Discovery Books
Macmillan Publishing Company
866 Third Avenue
New York, NY 10022

Maxwell Macmillan Canada, Inc.
1200 Eglinton Avenue East
Suite 200
Don Mills, Ontario M3C 3N1

Macmillan Publishing Company is part of the Maxwell Communication Group of Companies.

First edition
Printed in the United States of America

10 9 8 7 6 5 4 3 2 1

LIBRARY OF CONGRESS CATALOGING-IN-PUBLICATION DATA
Bandon, Alexandra.
Mexican Americans / by Alexandra Bandon. — 1st ed.
p. cm. — (Footsteps to America)
Includes bibliographical references.
Summary: An account of one of the largest groups of immigrants in the United States, with special
emphasis on the recent history of the group and including first-person narratives.
ISBN 0-02-768142-4
1. Mexican Americans—Juvenile literature. 2. Mexican Americans—History—Juvenile literature.
[1.Mexican Americans.] I. Title. II. Series.
E184.M5B36 1993   305.868'72073—dc20   92-41001

Contents

Part I

The Land They Left Behind

== 1 ==

Why Do They Leave?

The First Mexican Americans

The United States has been built by immigrants who have flocked to North America since Colonial days. Yet for many years before the first Pilgrims landed at Plymouth Rock, Mexicans already lived in the Rio Grande Valley of what is now Texas. So the first Mexican "immigrants" to the United States were not really immigrants at all. As aborigines and descendants of the conquistadores, they were residents of the part of Mexico that became United States territory after the Mexican-American War. Indeed, what is now California, New Mexico, Arizona, Texas, and Colorado was once all part of a very large Mexico.

In 1821 Mexico declared its independence from the Spanish colonial rule that had existed for 300 years. Twenty-four years later the United States annexed the fledgling Republic of Texas, ending nine years of Texan independence. Then, with the Treaty of Guadalupe Hidalgo, signed in 1848 to end the Mexican-American War, and the Gadsden Purchase of 1853, the United States acquired territory constituting nearly half of Mexico. The Mexican residents of this land became the first Mexican Americans.

Mexican Americans go by many names in America. Mexicans who leave Mexico are emigrants, but when they get to their new country, they become immigrants (leaving a country is

Mexican laborers picking cotton on a Texas plantation in 1919. Many of the first Mexican immigrants worked as seasonal agricultural laborers.

emigrating; coming to a country is immigrating). Once they establish themselves as residents of the United States, they become Mexican Americans, and their American-born children become second-generation Mexican Americans, or Chicanos. All Mexican Americans are part of the larger group of Hispanics, which also includes Puerto Ricans, Cubans, Dominicans, South Americans, and all other Spanish-speaking people in the United States.

Much of the land transferred to the United States after the Mexican-American War was populated by wealthy Mexican landowners, or rancheros. The rancheros struggled to keep land that had been theirs for years as they suddenly became Americans. New American settlers, mostly northern Europeans or their descendants, moved into this area, and it wasn't long before they took most of the territory away from the rancheros, who became strangers in their own land. The rancheros called these Americans Anglos, a term that refers to any English-speaking American who is not of Hispanic, black, Asian, or Native-American descent.

Anglo settlers on the formerly Mexican land turned these areas into cattle ranches, cotton fields, and irrigated farms. They built fences around their big cattle ranges, and the Mexicans with smaller herds of livestock no longer had room to graze their cattle. Thus, the Mexicans were pushed out by the Anglo settlers.

Because the Anglos' industries also required a lot of workers, the Mexicans displaced from their own ranches were recruited to work as cattle drivers or field hands. At the same time, Anglo-Americans began mining, logging, and railroad enterprises in the Southwest, where local Mexicans were the closest and cheapest labor available (many white Americans did not want to see black slaves introduced into territories that did not yet have slavery). These first Mexican "immigrants" took advantage of these work opportunities.

1900-1964

In the 1800s Mexican emigration was small, even though opportunities in the United States seemed promising. Opportunities in Mexico were equally good, so Mexicans did not benefit from crossing the border into a new country. Most of the Hispanic laborers hired by Anglos in the 19th century were actually native to the areas in which they worked, or had moved from

other parts of the Southwestern United States. If they did come
from Mexico, they were migrant workers, people who came north
for seasonal work with the intention of returning to their own
country when the work was finished. The permanent Mexican-
American population in the Southwest thus remained relatively
small until the present, when Mexicans began leaving their country in greater numbers. Political problems raged in Mexico, where
European imperialists had reestablished themselves in the 1860s,
and many people fled during the revolutionary period of 1910 to
1917, when Mexico was engaged in bloody internal warfare that
compelled many of its citizens to flee to the United States for safety. At the same time, the promise of jobs on farms and in factories
that produced goods to serve the Allied cause in World War I guaranteed the immigrants a place in their adopted country.

The 1920s were particularly difficult for postrevolution
Mexico and particularly prosperous for the United States. Many of
the Mexican immigrants of this time were seeking some of this
wealth. They took temporary jobs in the United States, returning
occasionally to Mexico and sending money to their families there.

In 1929, however, a sudden stock-market crash caused a
period of economic devastation, known as the Great Depression, in
the United States and much of the rest of the world. Jobs were
scarce; farmers were paid by the government *not* to cultivate their
lands in an effort to cut down on surpluses. Agriculture and
industry no longer needed Mexican migrant workers, so Mexican
immigration to this country dropped dramatically.

Not only were the opportunities poor for Mexicans coming to
the United States, but the fear that Mexicans would "steal"

Americans' jobs created an atmosphere of fear and mistrust. At one point in the early 1930s this hostility led to the massive deportation of hundreds of thousands of Mexican Americans, many of whom were American citizens, and to the closing of the Mexican-American border. Ultimately, the 1930s saw one of the lowest rates of Mexican immigration in U.S. history.

By the end of the decade war had erupted in Europe, and industry boomed in the West because of the need to supply goods to the Allies in what eventually became World War II. Many jobs were created in both the United States and Mexico, and Mexicans had little reason to look to the north for work. Yet, once President Franklin Roosevelt declared war in late 1941, there existed a true labor shortage in the United States, and the Roosevelt administra-

Trailer truck loaded with Mexicans. They were imported into the United States as laborers between 1942 and 1964.

tion asked Mexico for help to meet its manufacturing needs.

In 1942 the United States and Mexico began what was called the Bracero program ("bracero" is Spanish for "laborer," and often refers to a Mexican worker in the United States) in an effort to lure Mexicans to perform manual labor in this country. Braceros, overwhelmingly male, came to work in factories, producing goods for the war effort, in railroad construction, and on farms whose workers had gone off to fight. These men did the work that women could not or were not allowed to do and often performed tasks that were deemed "too dangerous for Americans." The two countries drew up an agreement guaranteeing free transportation and food, good wages, safe working conditions, and sanitary living quarters for the workers, though employers did not always abide by these rules. In the first three years of the program alone, 167,000 Mexicans came north to work as braceros. The program remained in effect until 1964.

Current Immigration

Since the 1960s the rate of Mexican immigration to the United States has increased steadily, reaching enormous proportions in the 1980s and the first years of the 1990s. This massive immigration from Mexico is due to many factors, not least the substandard education programs in that country. However, the single most compelling reason for Mexican emigration to the United States stands out above all others: the search for work.

The Mexican economy has been worsening in the past few

decades. Mexican farmers have frequently abandoned their country's rural areas in search of work in the cities when drought or bad crops have ruined their farms. (In the early 1980s the average Mexican farmer made the equivalent of $500 per year, and this situation has not improved in the following decade.) Once in the cities, however, the farmers find that the job situation is not much better. Urban areas like Mexico City cannot accommodate all the migrants looking for jobs. Even for those who do find work, the daily minimum wage in Mexico is only about equal to the *hourly* minimum wage in the United States. Unable to make a decent living in their own country, these farmers travel to the United States in search of work, and more and more come to stay. Some come as illegal (often called undocumented) immigrants; others come as temporary seasonal workers.

One of the greatest misconceptions about the Mexican immigrants to the United States is that they are the poorest of the Mexican population. *This is not true.* Most of the ex-farmers leave behind homes and land that their families own, something stable to which they can return if need be. The poorest workers, on the other hand, may be less willing to make the trip across the border and may not feel comfortable taking a chance on work in the United States, lacking as they do some savings or security.

The ailing economy in Mexico is also bad for that country's rich. Many upper-middle-class and wealthy Mexicans come to this country so that their money can be better handled by U.S. banks and other investment firms. These people become professionals, businesspeople, or shop owners. Some, however, who give up high-status careers in Mexico for the chance of a better standard

A successful book shop owner and collector. Many Mexican immigrants make their livings as small-business owners.

Outskirts of
Morelia, Michoacan,
in Mexico. Poverty
and poor conditions
in Mexico drive
many Mexicans to
seek a new life in
the United States.

of living in America find (as do many immigrants educated outside
the United States) that credentials valid in their own country are
not always accepted in the United States. Often, Mexican-trained
doctors, lawyers, and architects cannot practice their professions
here because they are not certified by U.S. standards. Many of
these skilled people make money in the United States by working
in lower-status occupations than the ones they worked in in
Mexico. Yet most of them earn higher salaries as shop owners or
businesspeople in the United States than they did as doctors or
lawyers in Mexico.

Recently, unemployment in Mexico has reached new heights.
During the 1980s the unemployment rate was as high as 50 percent. That means that *half* the people able to work did not have
jobs. It's no wonder that many Mexicans travel to the United
States in search of opportunity. Even though this country has its
own unemployment problems, the chances for employment are still
better here for the unskilled Mexican worker.

In Mexico the job opportunities for unskilled workers are not
as vast as they are in this country. Here, there are so many more
factories and irrigation farms (which require more laborers than
so-called dry farms) that Mexicans seeking work here are likely to
find employment. Many of the jobs taken by Mexican immigrants
do not require high levels of skill or education, and newcomers
often work on production lines in factories; pick cotton, fruit, or
vegetables; do domestic jobs such as housekeeping or gardening;
or work in hotel and restaurant service. They labor in the manu-
facture of clothing and textiles; make parts for cars, planes, and
farm equipment. They also labor in food processing, electronics,

plastics, metal fabricating, and steel. Unfortunately, because these jobs require less skill and education than more complex tasks, they tend to pay less well. And though recent studies show that current Mexican immigrants are better educated than those who came a few decades ago, they still lag behind most Americans in skills and educational achievement.

The main reason for the high unemployment level in Mexico is overpopulation. The population of Mexico grows so quickly that it doubles every 27 years! Mexico cannot possibly accommodate the vast number of people entering its work force each year. It is estimated that there are 700,000 *new* workers in Mexico each year, but only 300,000 new jobs for them. Therefore, each year 400,000 people join the potential work force without any hope of finding work.

Overpopulation also contributes to poor living conditions for many Mexicans. In the cities, overcrowding combined with weak environmental regulations leads to terrible pollution. In rural areas the roads remain unpaved, and the regular travel required for migrant work is difficult.

Thus, many Mexicans make the difficult decision to leave a place they have known all their lives and try a new existence in a country where the language is strange and the culture is markedly different. Not every emigrant to the United States is eager to leave his or her country and become an American citizen, and the choice of countries to which Mexican emigrants can travel is large. Yet most Mexicans who leave their country come to the United States, the land just north of the border.

Eduardo Fuentes
Crossing the Border

Eduardo Fuentes is a college student at the University of Southern California. He is 29 years old.

I'm older than most of the students here. It took me longer to get here because I had a longer way to go.

I didn't have a care in the world when my father was alive. It seemed that there was nothing he couldn't fix with a warm smile or a pat on the back. Back then it didn't seem to matter that we lived in a one-room shack or that we ate rice and beans when we were lucky enough to eat. But that safe world of my childhood ended when my father died, just before my 13th birthday.

With me and my brother, Jaime, to feed, my mother tried to find work. But there were no jobs to be had. I saw that little by little she gave up hope. So when I was 13, I decided we would leave Mexico and move to America. But we wouldn't go like ignorant people with blind hope, I decided. We would plan.

I started to study English every night with a neighbor. I saved every penny I could from the job I had unloading vegetables at the market. My mother took in sewing. Then an uncle loaned us a little money. It took us three years, but we were ready.

We took the bus to Tijuana from Oaxaca, our city in the South. When we got to the border, dusk was just falling. I couldn't believe how many people were there, waiting to cross. I helped my mother find a place to sit. I bought sodas and tacos for her and Jaime.

My mother had left all the decisions to me, but I didn't mind. The neighbor who had taught me English had a sister in Los Angeles who would help us. I was sure that good things would happen. I would make them happen.

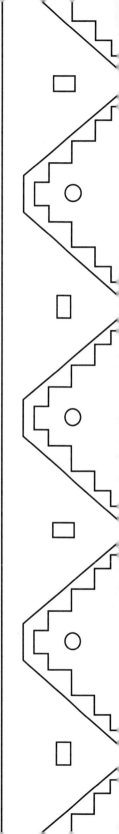

When darkness fell, people started drifting toward the river or searching for other places to try their luck getting across. I picked a guide who looked trustworthy, and he promised to lead us across the Rio Grande and toward the right road. He sold me plastic bags and rubber bands so that we could cover our feet and protect them from the river.

We walked for about a mile in the darkness. Finally the guide said that this was the place to cross. I took my mother's elbow. She was holding Jaime. She and I had packs strapped to our backs. The water felt greasy, and even though it was warm, it made me shiver. We moved quickly, following the guide. In only minutes we were standing on the other bank in the United States.

The guide told us to wait, then he ran up the bank. I could feel my mother shaking with fear beside me. We waited in the darkness, scared our guide wouldn't return. Finally he came back and motioned us up the riverbank. But as we reached the top a truck suddenly roared out of nowhere, its headlights blazing white. It was the border patrol.

The guide quickly hustled us behind a group of low bushes. We crouched down, breathing hard. Jaime began to snuffle, as if he was about to cry. He had to be quiet, so I gave him a piece of candy that I'd brought along for just that purpose. He calmed down, and the guide gave me a relieved look. The truck finally drove off.

"Okay," the guide said after a minute. "We can go."

We walked across a hard-packed field and came to a road. The road led to a big highway.

"This is Interstate Ten," the guide said. "You can cross it, but be careful. The cars are going faster than you think. Follow the road over there and it will take you to a bus station."

I paid the guide the rest of the money. I looked at the big American highway. The cars were going so fast! My mother's eyes were wide with fear. But this was the way we had to go.

I took Jaime from my mother's arms. I watched the road, waiting. Then I called, "Now!" and we ran as fast as we could. Even though I had been careful, I saw bright headlights coming at us out of nowhere just as we were halfway across. We leaped the last inches just as the car swerved to the far lane. My mother fell to the grass of the median. I sat beside her and we tried to catch our breath. Jaime started to cry and wouldn't stop.

There were other people on the median, too scared to try again. But I knew we had to cross. There would be border patrol guards checking the highway. I pulled my mother to her feet and held Jaime against my chest. The traffic was worse on this side. I was squinting against the headlights, waiting for our chance. When I saw an opening I pulled my mother across the highway. She was sobbing and terrified. Cars zoomed toward us and crossed to another lane, honking at us. A truck driver blared his horn at us and kept going. He wouldn't change lanes, so we had to jump the last few feet to safety. We felt the wind from the truck against our backs.

But we were safe. I laughed out loud. My mother looked at me as though I was crazy. "Now all we have to do is follow the road to the bus," I told her. "We're together. We made it. The worst is over."

Of course, the worst was yet to come, but I didn't know that. There were so many bad days in the beginning. Before we made it to Los Angeles we had to sleep in bus stations for two weeks. Then once we arrived my mother fell sick.

But good things happened, too. I'm graduating this year with a degree in business. My mother works in a dress shop. Jaime is a good student. We are all American citizens. We made it. And we are together.

⫤ 2 ⫥

Why the United States?

Migrant Workers

S ome Mexicans who emigrate to this country do so with no intention of staying. They are looking for temporary work that can help them earn money to support themselves back in Mexico. They usually have a stable life in Mexico that they are reluctant to abandon. They are motivated by the chance to earn better money in jobs that are more readily available in the United States.

Though fewer and fewer Mexicans are performing migrant work here with the intention of returning to Mexico when the job is through, many do still come to the United States as temporary laborers, leaving their families behind. This arrangement benefits both the many U.S. manufacturers whose production is seasonal and the Mexican workers who wish to be near to home so that sending their earnings to their families will not be difficult. The Mexican government does nothing to discourage this migration, as the money these Mexicans send home helps their country's poor economy.

Many migrants work very hard during their time in the United States, then return to Mexico in the off-seasons to enjoy their families and friends. Their whole year's wages are dependent upon the months they spend working in the North. And for their own part, the farmers and manufacturers who hire Mexican migrants are dependent upon their regular return each year.

This dependence, however, does not always ensure that the U.S. employers treat the migrants fairly. Many migrants are over-worked and underpaid. And because many do not speak English well, are unfamiliar with the organizations and laws that might help them, or are undocumented workers afraid of being deported, they are slow to take action to improve their situation.

The Country Next Door

In the past, especially in the period from the 1920s to the 1950s, most Mexicans working in this country were migrants. Over time, though, more and more Mexicans became permanent immigrants. The United States' proximity to Mexico is still this country's primary appeal to these Mexican immigrants, for whom leaving their homes is not only heartbreaking but expensive. Leaving Mexico in any manner other than land travel or the rela-tively inexpensive plane trip to the United States is too costly for many Mexicans. Though many employers around the world recruit foreign workers (Saudi Arabian and Kuwaiti oil companies hire for-eigners to work in the oil fields; wealthy families from Italy and Hong Kong, among other places, often employ foreigners in domes-tic service), Mexicans seldom travel farther than the nearby United States. For many Mexicans this is the only country to which they can afford to emigrate without leaving their families too far behind, and many Mexicans now bring their families with them. And the sharp contrasts between life on the two sides of the border—often, barren and desolate Mexican territory faces a thriving city on the U.S. side—draws Mexicans to the United States.

For Mexican workers trying to enter this country illegally, the close border allows multiple entry attempts (often several tries in one day) when the border patrol is especially watchful. Sneaking past the border, however, is a relatively recent phenomenon, dating back only a few decades.

Until recently, the United States had few limits on Mexican immigration. Before 1929, in fact, unrestricted immigration was allowed from Mexico. At a time when boatloads of European immigrants were made to pass through a clearinghouse on Ellis Island, where lack of the proper identification papers or poor health might cause them to be detained or even deported, Mexican immigrants were driving or walking across the border with no one examining

Jaime Escalante, teacher at Garfield High School in California and subject of the movie Stand and Deliver. *Escalante has helped many students go to college despite prejudices .*

them at all. All they had to do to cross the border was pay five
cents! Travel between Mexico or Canada and the United States was
unmonitored to the point that immigration figures from the turn of
the century did not even count arrivals from our neighbor countries.

In the 1930s, however, during the Great Depression, Americans became sensitive to Mexicans immigrating in search of jobs. Still, it wasn't until the enactment of the 1965 Immigration Act that Congress placed a cap on the number of people who could enter from Mexico, and even then the restriction was vague, since it did not specify a limit for the country of Mexico alone but set a single figure (120,000 people) for *all* the countries of the Western Hemisphere combined. Not until 1976 did an amendment to this act limit Mexican immigration to 20,000 people annually.

Mexican Networks and Culture

Another compelling reason Mexican emigrants choose to move to the United States is the number of Mexicans already living here. These established Mexican Americans often help immigrants find homes and jobs. They also work to maintain a strong Mexican culture within the United States. Their unofficial programs of assistance, called networks, make the transition for new Mexican Americans more comfortable.

Many Mexicans look to relatives or friends they knew in Mexico who have already emigrated to the United States to lead them to jobs where they will be welcome, and sometimes the new arrivals have work and homes awaiting them here. (Quite often Mexican immigrants are allowed in this country only because they are directly related to Mexican-American citizens or permanent residents.) The earlier immigrants may act as translators for the newcomers whose English is not yet good. Or maybe they work in a factory where many Latinos work and where the new immigrant will feel welcome.

Once they arrive here some Mexican immigrants are happy to find that they can survive without knowing English perfectly and without giving up on the culture they left behind in Mexico. The first Mexican settlers who became American citizens after the Mexican-American War preserved their culture and traditions in their own neighborhoods or towns, often so closely that these areas looked like actual Mexican towns moved across the border. In the 19th century even the terrain that Mexicans inhabited in the United States looked like the land they had left behind. Irrigation and mechanization have made the American Southwest look different now, but 19th-century Mexicans found comfort in moving to a place very much like their own country and inhabited by many of their own countrymen.

As new immigrants arrived in these neighborhoods, or barrios, they replenished the culture with a constant influx of Mexican language and traditions. Immigration from Mexico has never dropped off enough to let the barrios become truly Americanized. Thus, though Mexican Americans are often more American than Mexican, there are still places in the United States where some of the residents speak only Spanish and where the shops carry only traditional Mexican goods. Near the border Mexican television and radio make their way over the airwaves into the United States, while many American stations cater to Mexican Americans. New residents have been known to complain that they have no one with whom to practice their English!

Recent immigration figures indicate that Mexican culture in the United States will continue to be maintained. In 1986

A pharmacy in East Los Angeles showing the extent of Mexican influence in the barrio

Congress passed new immigration laws, including a provision that gave amnesty to undocumented immigrants who had lived in the United States for a certain number of years or who were involved in certain agricultural work. Amnesty (a kind of pardon) is the government's way of letting undocumented workers get visas to stay in this country rather than be deported for breaking immigration laws. More than two million undocumented immigrants had the opportunity to apply for visas under this one-time amnesty, and two thirds of the 1.7 million undocumented immigrants given amnesty were Mexican.

Officials were surprised to see so many Mexicans eligible for amnesty because the law said that immigrants had to prove they had been living in the United States without pause for at least five years. Thinking that many undocumented workers were migrant laborers, the government believed that many fewer Mexicans than actually qualified had fulfilled that requirement.

With the addition of so many newly arrived Mexicans in recent years, the Mexican networks and culture in this country have been strengthened enough to accommodate even more immigrants. More Mexican Americans, especially those who received amnesty, will be sending for their families than in several of the previous years combined, and Mexican culture will thrive in the barrios.

Work Opportunities

Perhaps because of the enormous number of jobs available during World War II and through the Bracero program, the United States has retained an image as the country of streets paved with gold and jobs for everyone. Some of these images are not so far

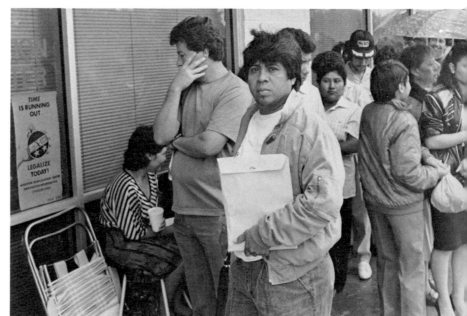

Hundreds of undocumented immigrants, many of them Mexican Americans, wait on April 29, 1988 — just five days before the deadline — to receive amnesty under the 1986 law.

from the truth. The streets of America may not be paved with
gold, but there are eight times as many cars per family driving on
them as there are in Mexico. There are also nine times as many
telephones and five times as many televisions, and Americans
spend eight times as much on educating their children, privately
and through taxes, as Mexicans do. Mexicans stream over the border in search of these benefits. Some find them, while others find
only hard, low-paying work and terrible treatment by employers.

As mentioned in the previous chapter, many Mexican Americans
find better-paying jobs here than they could in their native country.
Some earn 20 times as much as workers performing the same jobs
across the border. In addition, because of workers' unions in the United
States, many jobs here are more stable than they might be in Mexico.

We have already seen that many Mexicans come to the
United States for manufacturing and agricultural work. In the
past most of these workers were young men with little or no training or education. Recently, however, more women and children
have been traveling to the United States in search of work. With
the high rate of unemployment in Mexico, women and children are
often the last to get jobs there. Yet many families need the finan-
cial support of all their members, including mothers and children.
Thus, entire families, including grandparents and grandchildren,
are relocating to the United States so that a greater number of
their members can take advantage of the work opportunities here.
More than two thirds of Mexican immigrants live in this country
with their immediate families.

Many of the workers coming to the United States are coming
with skills acquired in Mexico from American training. In an
effort to produce goods less expensively so as to make a higher

A family from
Oaxaca, Mexico.
Recently, entire
Mexican families
have been immi-
grating to the
United States.

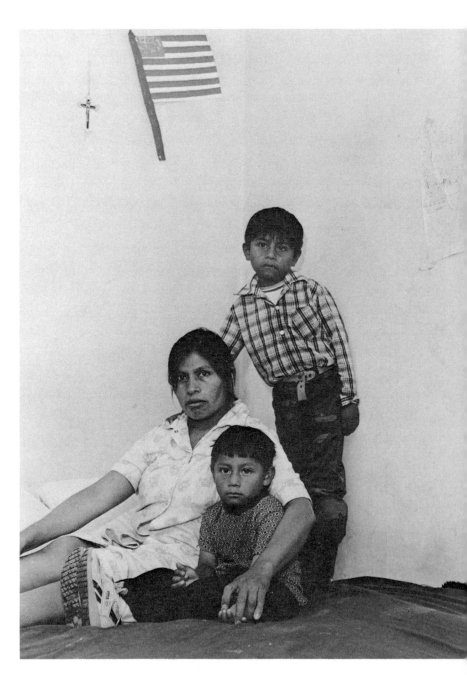

profit, some American companies have developed a system of *maquiladoras,* or "twin plants." These American manufacturers produce the parts for their goods in cities on the American side of the border and then send them to nearby cities on the Mexican side to be assembled. By creating these dual plants, which are often encouraged by local governments in both countries, the manufacturers hope to slow down illegal immigration.

The labor for assembly is much cheaper in Mexico than in this country, so the products end up costing less when the customer buys them in the store. And of course the manufacturer also makes more money by spending less on making the product. Furthermore, in the Mexican maquiladora plants, workers are trained in production and management, giving them, perhaps, the incentive to stay in Mexico, or at least providing them with the skills they need to get good jobs in the United States. Sometimes the creation of a maquiladora plant on the United States side does create new jobs for Americans, but the movement across the border of the assembly work can also take jobs away from U.S. workers, making it harder for them to buy goods, no matter how less-expensively made they may be.

=≡ 3 ≡=

What Is Their Journey Like?

Waiting for Visas

The United States uses a complex system to keep track of foreigners coming into this country, but the first document an immigrant needs is a visa. A visa lets immigration officials (from the Immigration and Naturalization Service, or the INS) know that the government has approved a certain person's entry into the country, either because that person is just visiting as a tourist, has work in this country, is looking to relocate to the United States and then find work, or is coming to live with relatives.

A nonimmigrant visa is issued to those people who want to come to this country temporarily. They must identify the reason they are coming (for example, to perform in a concert, to train with the American branch of the company they work for elsewhere, to attend school, or just to travel as a tourist). These visas have time limits on them, the length of which depends on the purpose of the visit. Nonimmigrant visitors must usually leave or renew their visas within a year (sooner if they are simply tourists), and they are only allowed to do that activity which their visas specify. A visitor on a tourist visa cannot work at all; a student may go to school but may not work; and a concert performer may only perform at the concerts specified to the INS. Visitors who overstay their nonimmigrant visas are in the United States illegally and are subject to deportation.

The other type of visa is an immigrant visa. Immigrant visas are for visitors who intend to move to the United States permanently because they have either jobs or family in the United States. Immigration laws rank the different reasons a person might immigrate in order of preference. Those who are sponsored by immediate family members (spouses, parents, or children) are given first preference; then come workers with talents the United States wants (artists, scientists, teachers, or performers with "exceptional" or "extraordinary" ability). Immigrants who are sponsored by other family members (siblings or siblings-in-law) are further down on the preference list. Unskilled workers have no place in the ranking; that is why Mexican laborers are more often sponsored by relatives than by employers. By establishing these preferences, the United States government announces which immigrants it feels are most desirable to have living in the United States. The government's stated preferences have changed over the years. Sometimes doctors are more in demand; other times it is the turn of skilled workers.

Since the passage of the Immigration Act of 1990, which went into effect in October 1991, there has been a *quota* for each level of the ranking system, including the level for immediate family members (who used to be allowed to enter the United States in unlimited numbers). These quotas are limits on the number of people who can get visas each year on each level. There are quotas for each country and there are quotas for all countries combined. Each country's share of the overall quota is determined by a complex process. In addition, there are separate quotas for rela-

tives of immigrants, employer-sponsored immigrants, and the relatives of the people granted visas under the 1986 amnesty. The 1990 act greatly expanded most of the work-related quotas but pared down the quotas on family members.

Mexicans need immigrant visas to live in the United States legally. Any foreigner trying to get an immigrant visa must bring to the American consulate (a local office of the embassy in his or her country): a birth certificate, a letter from the local police saying that he or she is not a criminal, and a passport. Would-be immigrants must also take physicals to prove they have no contagious diseases.

Unfortunately, there is often a long wait for an immigrant

visa, which must be obtained *before* coming to the United States.
Some Mexicans have been waiting as long as ten years for their
visas, though most wait only five years or less. Still, even a cou-
ple of years of uncertainty while waiting for a visa can be unbearable. And with the passage of the Immigration Act of 1990, which
eliminated a category in the preference system for immigrants who
have no sponsor, some people who have waited a long time are not
even eligible anymore.

Foreigners used to be able to come the United States without an employer or family connections. In 1980 there were
173,000 such Mexican visa applications waiting to be approved;
the 1990 estimate was around 250,000. However, since
Congress passed the 1990 act, there is only a very slim chance
that anyone can get a visa without a job or a relative in the
United States. People applying for visas because they want to
work in the United States must show that they have definite jobs
waiting for them here and that American citizens could not do the
jobs as well or better.

People trying to get family-preference visas must be directly
related to an American citizen or to an immigrant with a perma-
nent-resident, or "green," card. Green cards and citizenship are
available only to immigrants who are in this country legally.

However, when Congress granted amnesty to undocumented
immigrants through the 1986 act, it intended to keep families
together. In that cause, it set aside a completely separate quota
for the parents, children, and spouses of amnesty recipients.
These applicants do not have to meet any other requirements; they
should be granted visas immediately. Unfortunately, the waiting

list for Mexicans with family members in the United States is fuller than a single year's quota.

For relatives of legal immigrants (not amnesty recipients) the different types of family members seeking visas are ranked. Spouses, children, and parents get priority; male siblings and siblings-in-law may have to wait years before getting a visa. Each ranking gets a quota, some larger than others, and the category as a whole has a combined quota.

Each category—work-related visas, family-member visas, and amnesty recipients' visas—has its own annual quota. As each quota is filled, the people who did not get visas have to wait another year, or as many years as it takes, until their names get to the top of the list. That means that if the annual quota is 50,000 and there are 150,000 applicants, the last people on the list would not get into this country for three years, even if they meet all the visa requirements immediately. That is why there is such a long wait for Mexicans trying to get into the United States. As a result, many Mexican Americans who send for their relatives, especially the more than one million who were granted amnesty under the 1986 law, find that there just aren't enough spaces each year to get them here.

Some immigrants try a well-known trick to get an instant visa: They marry American citizens. Often, when two people marry in the United States just to get a visa for one of them, they do not even know each other. They may have been brought together by an intermediary, who is paid for the introduction. The immigrant pays to marry an American, and in return gets a chance to stay here. However, many of these false marriages are discovered, because the INS has a careful interview system to detect such arrangements. The immigrant who gets caught in a sham marriage is immediately deported and will probably never be allowed back into the United States; the American participant could face a severe fine or even time in jail.

Illegal Entry

Because the wait for visas can be so long, many Mexican immigrants choose to skip the formalities and try to enter the United States illegally. Some remain after tourist visas have run out; others sneak across the border. Though immigrants without visas are generally referred to as "illegal," they are actually some of this country's most law-abiding residents. Aside from their illegal entry, their crime rate is lower than that of American citizens, possibly because they fear being deported. Some people prefer to describe these immigrants as undocumented.

As many as four million Mexicans cross the border illegally each year, yet only one fourth of them are caught. Many are caught repeatedly as they try over and over to gain entry. The possibility of such multiple attempts is available only to Canadians and Mexicans. Unlike other foreigners, they do not need to depend on a boat or plane ride, where their time and place of entry into the United States would be registered. They need only wait at the border until the right moment arrives to evade the U.S. guards and sneak in.

If caught, illegal immigrants are not arrested. They are just sent back to their country, where they can try again and again until they succeed in getting into the United States. The border patrol freely admits that a Mexican or Canadian who tries long enough to cross the border will eventually get through. (Ninety percent of all the undocumented immigrants caught in the United States are Mexican.)

The Mexican-American border is 1,936 miles long, but is patrolled by only 3,000 border guards. Still, so much of the border area is marked by barren desert, canyons, impassable woods, or rivers (see map) that there are only seven main crossing points. Almost three quarters of the illegal crossings happen near Chula Vista, California, and the ten-mile stretch of border at El Paso, Texas.

Mexicans wanting to enter this country without being caught usually arrive near the crossing point in the early evening just before dark. On any given evening they can be seen waiting patiently for night to come in the fields or on the riverbanks on the Mexican side of the border. When darkness falls they dash to the U.S. side through holes in the wire border fence or through the shallow waters of the Rio Grande.

In the meantime the Border Patrol waits on the U.S. side, tracking the illegal immigrants' movements. Many will be stopped and driven back to Mexican land, where they may make anther attempt at crossing the border the very same night, or the next day.

Many would-be immigrants put their lives in the hands of coyotes—people who are paid to smuggle Mexicans across the border. The Mexicans pay hundreds of dollars, sometimes a life's savings, to be taken directly to a city where jobs are waiting. These trips are hard: The coyotes have been known to pack dozens of people into one truck without air-conditioning or even ventilation. They do not care about their passengers, just about their money.

(continued on page 43)

Undocumented immigrants wading the Rio Grande to avoid being caught by Border Patrol agents. Up to four million undocumented Mexicans cross the border each year.

Alicia Cabrera
In The Hands Of A Coyote

Alicia Cabrera owns her own plant-nursery business in San Diego, California. She came to the United States illegally with her mother when she was 12 and is now an American citizen.

I didn't even want to go to America. I remember sobbing and clinging to my grandmother until my mother pulled me away from her. We were going to San Diego to live with my Uncle Mario and my Aunt Elena, relatives I had never even met. They had promised my mother a job in their business. They had a big house with plenty of room and they said we could live with them as long as we wanted or needed to.

It was a generous offer, and my mother couldn't refuse it. Still, it was hard for me to leave all my relatives. I cried so much my grandmother told me I could water her whole garden. I couldn't even laugh, I was so sad.

My mother gave the last of her savings to a coyote, a man who would drive us past the border. He would take us to a bus station in San Diego, and Uncle Mario would pick us up there. Everything was arranged. But when the coyote arrived, something about his eyes frightened me. I whispered to my mother that he had dead eyes, but my mother told me to hush, that everything would be okay. We climbed into the van, which was already crammed full of people. We squeezed into a tiny space. No one spoke as the van took off.

I remember holding on to my mother's hand while the van bounced over the road. It was dark and hot, and I was poked by an old woman's bony hip every time the van hit another hole. The trip seemed to take forever. I lost track of time. Then, suddenly, the van jerked to a halt. Someone thanked God that the hot ride was over. We heard a door slam up front. We waited, but nothing happened.

Someone spoke. "Maybe he stopped for gas."

"Or a cold drink."

"If only *I* had a cold drink," a young man with a drooping mustache said, and a few people laughed.

We waited in silence for something to happen. The minutes stretched on. Then people started to talk in low voices. Were we in San Diego? Was the man coming back? Should we try the door? Someone said it was dangerous, and someone else said we should try anyway.

Finally the young man with the mustache said that the children were suffering, that we had to try the door. My mother reached over and pushed and pulled. Then the young man tried.

The door was locked.

The young man cursed and then apologized. I remember how the sweat dripped off his mustache. I looked around and realized that everyone else was sweating, too. My mother's hand was wet against mine, but we didn't let go. It was so hot in the van that I could hardly breathe.

Someone yelled, "Let us out!" and then everyone was shouting. We pounded and pounded on the walls of the van, but nothing happened. Then we lay back, even more exhausted and hotter than before.

I remember staring at the grownups in the van, realizing that no one knew what to do. At some point I must have fallen asleep. I kept dreaming of cool water.

When I woke up it was still dark. It was too hot to talk. Someone had a little water, and we shared it, taking tiny sips. Every once in a while someone would yell and pound on the side of the van. But then no one had the strength anymore. My mother was praying softly. I would drift off into a dream, then wake up. I would touch my mother's skirt and fall asleep again.

After a long while the blackness turned to gray and the heat got even worse. The sun was up. We were roasting, like chickens in my grandmother's oven. I wondered if the air itself could burst into flame.

Then I heard something. At first I thought it was a dream. But it was real. Footsteps.

The man with the mustache began to pound against the side of the van. He was weaker now, but still he pounded and pounded, as hard as he could. Anyone who could lift a hand pounded and pounded. I pounded and sobbed. The van rocked back and forth. I couldn't talk because my throat was too dry, but in my head I was screaming: Please let us out of here!

Someone yelled from outside that he would get us out. It felt like hours before we heard footsteps again. And then the door was opening. We crawled out slowly, one by one. No one's legs could support them, and we dropped to the ground like dead flies. Some people didn't get out at all, but lay inside, limp. I stumbled out and fell. I found myself staring at a pair of dusty cowboy boots.

"Oh, my God," a voice said above me.

They took us to the hospital. My mother and I were luckier than most; we were released a few days later and went home with Uncle Mario. A three-year-old baby had died in the van.

The night we left the hospital, I slept under smooth sheets in the home of my aunt and uncle. The windows were open and a cool breeze stirred the curtains. My mother slept in the next bed. A pitcher of water sat on the table between us. Everything was peaceful and cool. But I dreamed of the coyote's dead eyes.

Many years have passed since that terrible day. The United States has been good to me. I've made many friends here and I have my own business. But sometimes, in some Anglo eyes, I see a flicker, a tiny glimpse of what I had seen in my dreams that night.

This is what I see: In this country, to some people, I am less than nothing. I can be left to die without a thought or a prayer. It is a lesson I had not wanted to learn. It is a lesson I will never forget.

In 1968, 45 Mexicans were abandoned by a coyote in a locked truck in San Antonio, Texas. One person died and 12 others were hospitalized for heat exhaustion. Undocumented Mexican immigrants have been the victims of many such injustices at the hands of coyotes.

Finding a Place in the United States

Once the new Mexican immigrants have crossed the border they must still find a place to settle down and live. Some choose to stay in the areas near the border. Many cities and towns right on the Mexican border, such as San Diego in California, and El Paso, Laredo, and Brownsville in Texas, have large populations of Mexican Americans. Cities a little farther from the border, such as Phoenix, Arizona; Los Angeles, Fresno, and San Jose in California; and San Antonio and Houston in Texas, are also home to millions of Mexican Americans. Other immigrants follow routes toward available work and move on to cities in the Pacific Northwest or on the Great Lakes.

The first Mexican Americans occupied a fan-shaped area near the Mexican border. Most were never really more than 150 miles from their native country, though their settlements stretched the full 1,936 miles along the frontier. At the time of the Treaty of Guadalupe Hidalgo in 1848, there were 5,000 Mexicans in Texas, 1,000 in Arizona, 7,500 in California, 60,000 in New Mexico, and smaller numbers in isolated settlements in Colorado. These settlers usually gathered in clusters near United States troops so that their towns would be easily defended against the Apaches and other Native Americans in the area. Later this pattern of settlement became a guide for new settlers, most of whom headed toward the areas already occupied by Mexican Americans.

When the two world wars created new, industrial jobs, many Mexican Americans who had been working as farmhands went to the cities, hiring on at steel mills and other plants that made products for the war. They lived in Chicago, Detroit, and other industrial cities in the Upper Midwest. Once Mexican Americans established themselves in these cities, barrios formed and more immigrants settled in them. Currently, 85 to 90 percent of

A Mexican American working in construction. Contrary to common belief, most Mexican Americans seek work in cities and not on farms.

Mexican Americans live in cities.

At the same time, other farm laborers who persisted in migrant agricultural work eventually created Mexican-American settlements in Washington and Oregon and in many parts of the South. Having already settled in parts of the Pacific Northwest in their days as miners and livestock herders, Mexican Americans today find it easy to create new settlements there. The movement into the South, largely for farm work, is more recent.

Once in the United States, undocumented immigrants tend to settle in cities and work in factories. Cities such as San Antonio, Los Angeles, El Paso, and Chicago are home to millions of undocumented Mexican Americans. Ninety-seven percent of the undocumented workers deported from Los Angeles (which has the highest number of undocumented immigrants of any American city) are Mexican.

Becoming a Citizen

An immigrant who arrives in this country is not automatically guaranteed a permanent place here, even if he or she has a visa. There are many steps to becoming a permanent resident and even more to becoming a citizen. Obtaining a visa is only the first requirement, and a Mexican immigrant may have to wait more than seven years after coming to the United States before becoming a citizen.

An immigrant with a visa may apply for a resident-alien card (a green card). Green cards are available only to those with immigrant visas—those who have been sponsored by their families or who have legally obtained permanent jobs. Immigrants with green cards must carry them at all times and report their current address to the INS once a year.

Mexicans wanting to become U.S. citizens must fulfill the same requirements as other immigrants. They must have lived in the United States for five years or be married to a United States citizen and have lived here three years. They must be over 18 and be able to speak, read, and write English at a certain level of fluency, though this requirement may be waived for would-be citizens who are 50 years old and have lived in the United States for more than 20 years. Candidates must pass a test on American history, which might also include basic questions on the Constitution and the government.

Before immigrants take this test, however, they must fill out citizenship-application forms, which are long and complex; sometimes, immigrants need help completing them. After the forms are returned to the INS a person may wait anywhere from six months to two years before he or she is contacted to attend a preliminary hearing, where an oral test is administered and suitability for citizenship is determined. As the applicant has already been in this country for at least five years, he or she has waited as many as seven years to become a citizen!

Once the immigrant passes the test, a petition for naturalization is filed on his or her behalf. Within a few months the immigrant will be contacted to attend a final hearing, where he or she is sworn in as a citizen. Citizenship candidates take an oath of loyalty to the United States, swearing that they will support and defend the Constitution (it is much like the oath the president takes!). Afterward, these new Americans can vote, take jobs that require citizenship, and bring their relatives into the country more

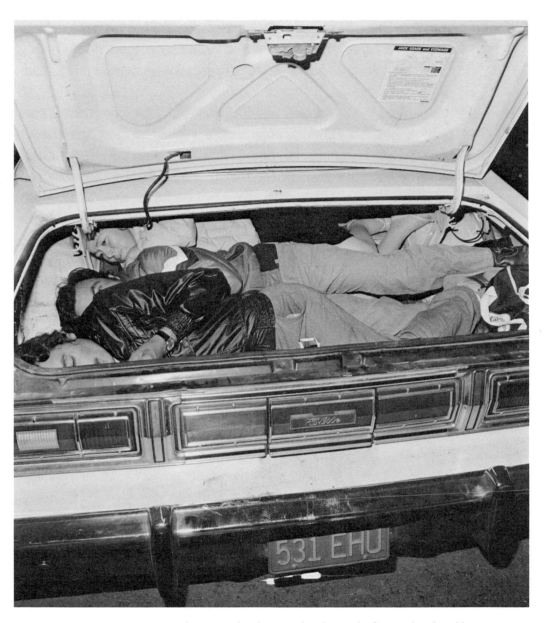

Indocumentados discovered in the trunk of a car abandoned by a coyote. Abuse by coyotes is one of the hardships Mexicans trying to enter the United States may endure.

easily. They have all the rights of natural-born citizens: They needn't carry a green card or notify the INS of their whereabouts, and they can obtain an American passport—one of the most desirable in the world.

Though the journey of Mexican Americans from their native country to the United States does not bring to mind the classic images of the American immigrant—a hopeful refugee huddled standing on the docks at New York City's Ellis Island—it is still an affecting picture. The unbearable wait for visas, the life's savings spent to pay a coyote, the horror stories of Mexicans left to die as they are smuggled across the border, the undocumented aliens' constant fear of deportation: These are all hardships a Mexican immigrant might have to endure in an attempt to secure a better life in the United States.

Part II

In the United States

= 4 =

Prejudices and Solutions

The Origins of Prejudice
Against Mexican Americans

The original Mexican Americans were closely involved in the creation of the new states of the Southwestern United States. They contributed to the composition of the state constitution of Texas, and passed laws in Texas, Colorado, and New Mexico requiring that governmental documents had to be printed in both English and Spanish. However, as they were slowly pushed off their lands by Anglo settlers, they lost much of their political power. This was the beginning of the prejudice and discrimination that Mexican Americans have faced in the United States. Without property or wealth, Mexican Americans were unable to preserve their self-determination and their voice in government.

In Texas and surrounding areas hatred toward Mexicans was particularly strong. Mexicans were still considered "the enemy": The hostilities of the Mexican-American War had not been forgotten. Anglos viewed Mexicans as cowards, compared especially to the brave fighting men who had defended the Alamo. In truth, though, these Anglo Texans were forgetting that Mexicans had fought beside them *inside* the Alamo as well as against them, and that the hard work of Mexican migrants had built the irrigation systems that had transformed parched Texas desert into rich agricultural land.

Moreover, many Anglo Texans had migrated from the South, where they had grown up with slavery and racial prejudice. Dark-skinned Mexicans were an easy target for the bigotry of these former residents of slave states, who had no qualms about stripping the power and land from people they considered inferior.

In New Mexico, Mexican Americans were spared this abusive treatment for a longer time, mainly because there was such a large number of them there. There were 60,000 Mexicans in New Mexico when it was annexed by the United States in 1845, vastly more than the number of Anglo settlers there. As Mexican Americans in other territories saw their power taken from them, those in New Mexico enjoyed many years of political influence because the Anglos there had always accepted them as equals. They had time to develop their own institutions, which became an important part of the state's organization. It was only when Anglos from other parts of the Southwest moved into New Mexico, bringing their prejudices with them, that the Latinos of New Mexico faced discrimination. In 1912 some members of Congress even fought against New Mexican statehood because there were so many Mexicans there who they felt were not deserving of American citizenship. Even so, the attitude toward Mexican Americans in New Mexico has never been quite as cruel as in the other southwestern states.

Elsewhere the treatment of Mexican Americans at the hands of Anglos varied. In the 1800s, California Mexicans were stereotyped as warm, charming, graceful, and full of happiness. Many of the Mexicans living on the coast of California had traded more with New England sea merchants than with other Mexicans and had little trouble adjusting to the ongoing presence of Anglos. In Arizona the Mexicans who had settled before the 1800s had died in battles with the Apaches or been chased out by them. When the Anglos arrived there were very few Mexicans remaining, and those who came later, brought in as miners, met with much the same hostility directed toward Texan Mexicans.

In some places Mexicans were considered an inferior "race." Many Mexicans are of mixed Spanish-Indian blood, or *mestizo.* They have darker skin and broader features than the pure Spanish who were Mexico's rulers in the 19th century, and they look even less like their unfriendly Anglo neighbors. Prejudiced Anglos in the United States used these physical differences as an excuse to say that the Native-American blood in Mexicans made them inferior. Later, during U.S. deportation campaigns, their unique appearance proved dangerous for many Mexican Americans.

Modern Prejudices

As railroads were built across the United States, more and more Anglos arrived in areas that were once largely or exclusively Mexican. They came in such great numbers that Mexicans quickly became a minority in most states. A few Mexican Americans emerged to act as intermediaries for the Anglo bosses and the Mexican workers. They became foremen, transporters, and business recruiters. They learned skilled crafts, worked as clerks, or opened businesses, such as restaurants or stores, that catered to the Mexican communities. However, because these enterprising Mexicans needed the support and trust of the frequently preju-

United States Army Master Sergeant Roy P. Benavidez, special forces, Green Berets. Benavidez is the recipient of the Congressional Medal of Honor, the highest medal awarded to military personnel.

diced Anglos, they were successful only on a limited scale.

In 1930 Mexicans were listed as an individual race on the census. In parts of the Southwest, Mexican Americans faced segregation much like that endured by blacks in the South. Many schools did not accept Mexican American children, using the excuse that Mexican children with a "language handicap" needed to be "Americanized" before they could be properly educated. Mexican Americans were also barred from voting by English literacy tests and poll taxes. (Eventually, the Supreme Court ruled that literacy requirements based solely on English are unconstitutional; the poll tax, a flat fee required from each person who wished to vote—and which was often and deliberately too expensive for blacks or Mexican Americans to pay—was eliminated by the 24th Amendment to the Constitution.) Signs saying NO DOGS OR MEXICANS ALLOWED were not uncommon in the Southwest.

This kind of discrimination led to one of the worst periods in Mexican-American history. Because of the Great Depression, which lasted throughout the thirties, many Americans were out of work and worried that Mexican workers would steal any jobs that were available by working for less money. Local police departments in the border states, particularly in Texas, began stopping people who even *looked* Mexican and driving them across the border into Mexico. Not only was this illegal, but many American citizens were mistaken for undocumented aliens and included in this mass deportation.

Others were cut off from the welfare program that was helping the rest of the country. Mexican Americans applying for welfare were directed to phony agencies whose sole purpose was to deport them. The rights of Mexican Americans were horribly violated during the 1930s; it is estimated that 250,000 people were sent out of the country in these brutal roundups.

World War II created jobs for many Mexican Americans and brought more of them in contact with Anglos in factories and in the army. In fact, a larger percentage of Mexican American than Anglo men fought in the war—300,000 to 500,000 Mexican Americans served during World War II—and many of them earned medals for their bravery (37 percent of all Medals of Honor went to Hispanic soldiers). Perhaps they joined the army in greater proportions than Anglos in an effort to prove their loyalty to the United States. Nonetheless, Hispanic servicemen saw more of the world during the war and learned that the prejudice they endured at home was not the norm. When the war was over many Mexican American veterans went to college, supported by the G.I. Bill, which guaranteed them an education they might not have received otherwise. Many became professionals and managers. Others, who had replaced Anglo workers in the factories during the war, had meanwhile learned trades that were useful in the postwar era.

Yet attitudes did not change among Anglos. Mexican-American soldiers returning from the war were frustrated to find that the freedoms they had enjoyed in the army would not continue. They were still considered an inferior "race" and were treated as second-class citizens. Riots in Los Angeles and San Diego during the early 1940s had only fueled Anglo prejudice. The so-called Zoot Suit Riots, named for an extravagantly tailored style of clothing worn by some Mexican-American men at the time, were instigated by Anglo servicemen who picked fights with Mexican American dockworkers, and were only worsened by racist police officers. Yet newspapers reporters that the riots were caused by

the "violent Indian blood" of the Mexicans. They said that pachucos, members of Mexican-American youth gangs, were the cause of the riots. The press simply encouraged the false impression of many Anglos that Mexican Americans are all criminals.

Nevertheless, even during this period, Mexican braceros enjoyed prosperity because of the work available to them. By the early 1950s, however, the government realized that the program was not stopping illegal immigration as had been hoped. From 1954 to 1958 a new deportation program called Operation Wetback (*wetback* is a disparaging term for an illegal Mexican immigrant, one who has presumably swum the Rio Grande to enter the country) was put into effect by the federal government.

Once again, people were stopped if they even looked Mexican, and if they could not prove immediately that they were American citizens, they risked arrest and deportation. All in all, 3.8 million Hispanics left the country during this period, many of them forcibly removed without formal deportation proceedings. And just the *threat* of deportation was enough to send some of those millions over the border without official coercion. During this period, ironically, illegal immigration increased. Many of those deported slipped right back into the country.

Even today, blaming Mexican Americans for bad economic situations has not stopped. Many Americans argue that the millions of undocumented workers in this country keep wages down because they accept lower pay (and take jobs away from American citizens). Of course, there *are* many jobs that undocumented workers hold that American citizens could perform, but employers often hire undocumented workers because they are the only ones willing to take certain jobs. And a 1980 census study prepared by the federal government showed that there is no connection among illegal immigration, unemployment, and low pay.

However, Americans continue to push for curbs on illegal immigration and both the 1986 and 1990 Immigration Acts were drafted with the intention of stopping undocumented workers from entering the country. All presidents and presidential candidates have always promised to do something about illegal immigration, because many American voters persist, despite evidence, in believing that undocumented workers cause unemployment to rise and wages to stay low.

Some experts believe that undocumented workers are actually *good* for the American economy, and argue that the low wages often paid them keep prices of goods and services low for all Americans. At the same time, by taking lower-rung jobs that many native-born Americans or legal immigrants refuse to accept, undocumented workers may push these others into higher-status and better-paying jobs. Furthermore, the presence of so many extra residents of the United States creates more jobs for teachers, salesclerks, health-care workers, and government employees.

Many Americans believe that undocumented workers come here to take advantage of federal programs like welfare, Medicaid, and Social Security. Actually, undocumented workers tend to use these social programs *less* than citizens or legal immigrants. They are usually afraid that by using them they will be discovered and deported. In addition, the money that undocumented immigrants pay in sales tax and in federal, state, and Social Security taxes withheld from their paychecks is more than the money spent on them when they *do* use these programs. Undocumented immigrants, who do not have Social Security numbers and therefore cannot file tax returns to get back any of this money or collect Social Security when they get older, end up paying proportionately more taxes than native-born citizens. Yet they don't benefit from the programs their taxes fund.

Perhaps surprisingly, many Mexican-American citizens and legal immigrants also resent the huge influx of undocumented Mexicans. They, too, point to job competition and worry that the undocumented workers' use of social services, especially schools, will weaken the effectiveness of these services for legal residents. This attitude is not new—it is the same attitude many onetime immigrants have had over the years toward new arrivals.

Lack of Political Control

One of the main reasons prejudice against Mexican Americans continues is that Hispanics lack political power. In

(continued on page 62)

Rosa Cisneros
"I'm an American!"

Rosa Cisneros is 73 years old and lives in Albuquerque, New Mexico. She is a retired accountant.

In 1935 I had a job in my Uncle Tino's drugstore, which was in the center of a small town near the border in Texas. It was in the middle of the depression, and times were bad. I remember that for my fifteenth birthday, my *quinceañera,* my grandmother made me a new red skirt. I was so proud of that skirt, so sure that it made me look very grown-up. I was very pretty then.

I knew I was lucky to be working in the drugstore, and I enjoyed it, too. I didn't even mind stocking shelves. I liked looking at the brand-new boxes and placing them in orderly rows. My favorite job was working behind the soda fountain. People came in for coffee or sodas, and there was always some gossip to hear and pass on.

I was born in Texas, but I couldn't speak English very well. I had lived all my life among my family, and Spanish was spoken everywhere. Only numbers made sense to me. Uncle Tino let me help with the account books, and he told me I had a head for figures. That was the first time I thought that maybe I could be something, have a profession.

One summer morning I walked to work early to avoid the heat. A car started to follow me. Two men sat in the front seat. I quickened my pace, even though it made my sandals dusty. I kept looking over my shoulder, getting more and more frightened by the minute. I didn't recognize these men, and I knew everyone in the neighborhood. They had flat, blank faces. They were Anglos, too. That scared me the most.

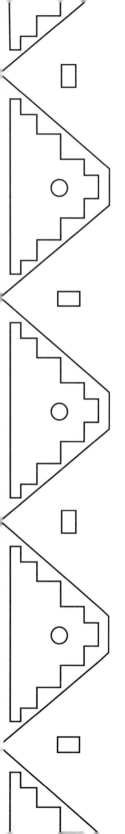

Suddenly the car accelerated and then pulled over toward me. The man in the passenger seat, who wore a cowboy hat, stuck his head out of the window and said, "Hey, señorita."

I didn't stop walking. I could hear the mocking tone in the man's voice.

"You'd better stop, little lady. Police." He flashed a badge, and I realized that the dark car was a police car.

I stopped. When the man asked me something in English, he spoke too fast and I didn't understand. I tried to stand straight and tall and look him in the eye.

"Get in," the other man, the driver, said in Spanish. "We're taking you back home."

I thought maybe something had happened to my family, so I got in the car. I was too scared to ask what was wrong.

But the men didn't circle around and go back to my house. They headed out of town. I asked them in Spanish where they were taking me. I was shy about my English and I didn't want to make a mistake. I was afraid that they would laugh at me.

"Back where you belong," the man with the hat said in English. *"Su casa. Comprende, señor-eeeta?"*

I said in slow, careful English that this wasn't the way to my house. It was back the other way, on Magnolia Street.

But I could see that the man didn't believe me. He asked me for identification, but of course I had nothing. I was just walking a few blocks to my uncle's store!

This time, I didn't say anything. That's what Uncle Tino had told me to do around Anglos. Times were hard then. We knew that many people resented Mexican Americans more than ever.

The man drove down a dusty road. I saw a sign: BORDER, 10 MILES.

I began to talk rapidly in Spanish, to explain that I was American, that my uncle expected me. I started to cry. The men didn't even look at me. They just kept driving.

I was still talking when we reached the Mexican border. The driver flashed some badge at the guard and drove right across. We drove on for a mile or so, then pulled over at a small store. The man with the hat reached behind the seat and opened my door.

"Vamos," he said. "Go home. And don't come back."

What could I do? I slid out of the seat. The car took off fast and I was left behind, choking in the dust the tires had kicked up. I had no money in my pocket and it was miles to my home. When I got to the border, I would have no papers to prove I should be allowed to cross back. I didn't feel like a grown-up woman anymore. I didn't feel pretty. I felt young and ugly and scared.

"I'm an American," I cried out. But nobody was there to hear me.

I'll never forget that day. Now, I remember it better than when I passed my CPA exam, or my wedding day, or even when my children were born. *That's* the day I remember.

relation to the size of the Mexican-American population, there are very few Hispanic political leaders to champion Mexican Americans' civil rights in the government. There are two main reasons why this is so: low voter registration among Mexican Americans and the frequently unfair design of voting districts.

Actually, as a group, Mexican Americans have a high voter turnout—four out of five eligible to vote do so. But many Mexican Americans cannot vote because many of them have never gone through the process of becoming citizens. On average, Mexican immigrants take longer to become citizens than do

immigrants from other countries, and of course a person must be a citizen to vote. Perhaps the delay in applying for and receiving citizenship is due to the closeness of Mexico, causing Mexican Americans to be slow to give up their original citizenship just as they are slow to give up their native customs. This is not a uniquely Mexican phenomenon—Canadians take just as long on average to become citizens, also apparently because the United States is so close to their original home. The more a Mexican American visits Mexico and maintains ties there, the less likely he or she is to become a citizen.

The requirements for citizenship, which include the ability to speak English and a knowledge of the American political system, may also keep some immigrants from becoming citizens. Some Mexican Americans believe there is no benefit to citizenship, that they already have sufficient rights and that they won't be paid any more in their jobs when they're citizens. In any case, the high number of noncitizen Mexican Americans and low number, therefore, of Mexican Americans who are registered to vote likely prevents many Hispanic politicians from reaching office. More Mexican Americans voting might mean more Mexican Americans in power.

The arrangement of voting districts is the second chief reason why Mexican Americans aren't well represented in politics. States, towns, and cities are divided into areas from which residents choose their particular political representatives, like a member of Congress or a state legislator. Often districts are designed in such a way that Mexican-American areas are split up and Mexican Americans never have a majority in any district. Sometimes politicians deliberately create districts in this manner to keep Mexican Americans out of power. Other times, though, local governments recognize the unfairness of this arrangement and redesign the voting areas so that minorities will have better representation.

Mexican Americans are missing from many key school positions, too. There are few Mexican-American school officials or teachers compared to the number of Mexican-American children. Since some of these positions are appointed by politicians, the lack of Hispanic school officials could be directly related to the shortage of Hispanic political leaders. Many Mexican Americans feel that their children are not getting the education they deserve because there aren't enough teachers and principals who can relate to them.

Recently strides have been made in Mexican-American politics. In 1981 Henry Cisneros became the first Mexican-American mayor of San Antonio, Texas, and, therefore, the first Mexican-American mayor of one of the ten most-populated U.S. cities. It was many years before Cisneros's election, however, that presidential candidates had first acknowledged the need to get the Mexican-American vote to be elected to office. John F. Kennedy campaigned strongly in 1960 to secure Mexican-American support with his "Viva Kennedy" slogan; as president, he openly voiced his thanks and returned the favor by giving political aid to many Mexican-American candidates. Every major presidential candidate since Kennedy has worked hard to win the Mexican-American vote: They know how important this group's support is to winning an election.

The Solutions

Long before Kennedy spoke to them about their potential contribution to politics, Mexican Americans were forming political and social groups in an effort to gain more power for themselves. Groups such as the American G.I. Forum, the Community Service Organization, the Mexican-American Political Association, and the Mexican-American Youth Organization paved the way for the Chicano movement that started in the 1960s and continues in a modified form today. Activists championed the Chicano experience and background, looking back to their Native-American origins as Aztecs, Mayans, and Toltecs. They promoted Americanism without abandoning their heritage. Many of these organizations still

Presidential candidate Bill Clinton with Mexican Americans in 1992. Politicians now recognize the importance of the Mexican-American vote.

exist and continue to fight for Mexican-American and Hispanic rights.

After World War II, Dr. Hector Garcia formed the American G.I. Forum when a cemetery in Texas refused to bury the body of a Mexican-American soldier killed in the war. With Garcia's efforts the body was eventually buried with full military honors in Arlington National Cemetery.

Working for Mexican-American civil rights, Garcia also fought for social programs like free school lunches and scholarships long before anyone else advocated them for Mexican-American students. He fought against segregation of Mexicans and was instrumental in bringing a discrimination case to the Supreme Court, which ultimately ruled that Mexicans had their rights violated as a class. Garcia named his group the *American* G.I. Forum to show that its members were American first. In 1984 President Ronald Reagan awarded Garcia the Medal of Freedom, the highest honor the president can bestow upon a civilian.

Currently the American G.I. Forum continues its work by helping Hispanics, particularly Mexican Americans, start or expand businesses, supports the study of Hispanic issues through scholarships and grants, and backs Hispanics seeking careers in politics or the media. It upholds its promise to "foster and perpetuate the principles of American democracy based on religious and political freedom for the individual and equal opportunity for all."

The Mexican-American Political Association (MAPA) was created in 1959 after the defeat of several Mexican-American political candidates left Hispanics frustrated. Many of the candi-

dates had lost largely because not enough Mexican Americans had
voted. By working for Mexican American legal equality and participation in politics, MAPA helped John F. Kennedy win the state
of Texas in the 1960 presidential election and helped elect many
politicians in California.

The Mexican-American Legal Defense and Education Fund
(MALDEF) was formed in 1968 to educate Mexican Americans
and other Hispanics in the workings of the American legal system and in how to protect their civil rights. MALDEF encourages young people to stay in school and works to get the funds
to the schools to keep them there. It provides scholarships,
especially for law-school students, and fights against culturally
biased testing. Currently MALDEF is battling discrimination in
businesses' hiring and promoting practices by challenging
English-only rules, and it is pushing for more Hispanic participation in politics. It is also working on behalf of Hispanic communities by making sure census counts are accurate and by
training future community leaders.

The Mexican American Women's National Association
(MANA) was founded in 1974 to work toward Mexican-American
and other Hispanic women's rights. MANA advocates many
Hispanic women's causes before Congress and local governments,
and it provides scholarships to undergraduate and graduate female
students. It works toward the economic and professional advancement of Hispanic women and trains them in leadership skills. It
also provides them with a chance to make contacts and find new
career opportunities through its many networks.

Dionicio Morales founded the Mexican American Opportunity
Foundation (MAOF) in 1960. In three decades of supporting the

Hispanic community, MAOF has continually adapted itself to meet new challenges facing the Hispanic world. It has designed programs to help Hispanic women, senior citizens, single parents, young professionals, and the unemployed. Its current programs are largely youth oriented, providing child-care services or referrals and funds for nutritional meals for children. MAOF also supports job training, a handiworkers' referral service, Spanish-language services and skills training for senior citizens, employment placement, and reading and writing lessons.

These organizations are just a few of the many groups formed to help Mexican Americans with their unique problems.

Cesar Chavez, August 1969. Chavez led the United Farm Workers in a strike against grape growers and alerted the country to the plight of the pickers, many of whom were Mexican Americans.

Through these associations Mexican Americans can take control over their own circumstances.

The Chicano Movement

During the 1960s a new group awareness developed among Mexican Americans following the lead of the black civil rights movement. The Chicano movement worked for the same civil rights that the American G.I. Forum and other organizations had championed. The Chicano, a contraction of *Mexicano* (which means "Mexican" in Spanish), was originally used to refer disparagingly to poor, lower-class Mexicans. During the 1960s, however, it became a word for positive ethnic identification. Chicanos asserted their pride in their Native-American background, their unique adaptation to American culture, and their language.

Among the many Chicano activists, three very different men stand out as leaders. In 1965 Rodolfo "Corky" Gonzales led *La Crusada para Justice*—The Crusade for Justice—by demonstrating against police brutality and the Vietnam War. Reis Tijerina gathered his supporters and occupied the Kit Carson National Forest in New Mexico to point out the claims the *Alianza Federal de Mercedes* had to the lands. And Cesar Chavez, the most famous of the three, led the movement for farm workers' rights.

Chavez was one of the founders of the United Farm Workers Union, which in 1965 organized a mass strike (*La Huelga*) by grape pickers in California, many of whom were Mexican American. Chavez showed the world how poorly these workers, many of them undocumented immigrants, were being treated by their employers. Some were being paid wages well below govern-

mentally recognized poverty levels. Chavez fasted to bring attention to the strike, and he organized marches and other nonviolent
demonstrations. He believed in peaceful change, much like
Mohandas Gandhi or Martin Luther King, Jr. In 1968 consumers
around the United States began boycotting grapes to support *La
Causa* (The Cause), and the grape industry suffered. *La Causa* was
noticed by everyone in America—Chavez was pictured on the
cover of *Time*, and his cause was supported by, among others,
Robert F. Kennedy. Ultimately, many growers gave in to the strikers' demands by paying them more and giving them benefits.

In the 1980s Chavez organized another strike and asked for
another boycott on behalf of grape pickers who were being
exposed to harmful pesticides. His slogan *"Viva la Causa"* ("Long
live the Cause") remains as inspiring today as it was in the sixties.

In 1969 and 1970 the National Chicano Moratorium
Committee organized demonstrations protesting the disproportion-
ately high number of Mexican Americans being killed in the
Vietnam War. The war was a particularly sensitive issue for
Chicanos because most of the soldiers were poor and uneducated
men who could not get out of the draft with a college deferment, as
did many more-affluent Anglos. That meant that a large number of
Mexican Americans were fighting and being killed in Vietnam at a
time when Mexican Americans had no equality at home.

On August 29, 1970, 20,000 people marched in East Los
Angeles in one of these protests, and police action against the
peaceful demonstrators instigated a riot. The police started the
fighting with the excuse that shoplifting and bottle throwing had
gone on a few blocks away from the demonstration; they preyed on
Anglo fears that Mexican Americans were all violent criminals.
Four hundred people were arrested, 100 were injured, and 3 died,

including a prominent *Los Angeles Times* reporter named Ruben Salazar, who was killed by a tear-gas shell fired at his head. To this day Chicanos see the Moratorium Riot as an inspiration to continue the fight to end prejudice against Mexican Americans.

The Chicano movement was part of the larger political-awareness process that for many people came and went with the sixties, but its effects are still with Mexican Americans. By defining Mexican Americans as an ethnic minority with rights, Chicano leaders opened the way for a new image of Mexican Americans as an important political and social minority.

United Farm Workers Union strikers in August 1969. Many Americans rallied to support the (mostly) Mexican-American grape pickers.

Teresa Martinez
The Barrio

Teresa Martinez lives in Los Angeles. She is a lawyer specializing in civil rights cases.

I grew up in the barrio. I was an average student most of the time. School was just a place to put in time. When I turned sixteen I thought about dropping out, maybe getting married or getting a job in the garment factory where my mother worked. My mother argued with me, telling me that I could do better, but I didn't care. I found it hard to care about anything. Already, at sixteen, I had seen so many try and fail. Nobody made it out of the barrio.

My father was a prime example. He had started out as a farm worker and had worked with Cesar Chavez back in the 60s. All I heard about while I was growing up was *La Causa*. So what? I would think. By the time I entered high school, my father had a job selling produce in the open-air market. He got up before the sun rose and came home smelling of rotten vegetables. What was the good of trying when you end up worse than you started?

Then one day everything changed. My mother died. There was a fire in the factory where she worked. It roared through the building in minutes. The fire doors had all been locked, "to prevent theft," the owner claimed. Bodies had been found huddled against the fire doors. They'd been trying to breathe air through the crack.

Whenever I thought of my mother's death, I thought of her crushed against that door, the door that shouldn't have been locked, the door that had trapped her inside an inferno. I kept imagining her beating against that locked door.

The injustice of what happened to my mother haunted me. I didn't sleep. I couldn't eat. At last my father sat me down and said: "You must do something or you will die." And finally I saw that he was right.

I began to study. I got a scholarship to college and then one to law school. I worked very hard, and when I graduated, I was offered a job in a big law firm in downtown L.A. I was also offered a job in the barrio, working with a small firm that specialized in civil-rights cases.

I was flattered that the big law firm wanted me. They took me to lunch in a fancy restaurant. Four men in beautiful suits sat around the table, eating expensive fish. They were glad to have someone of Mexican descent working for them, they said. They promised me interesting cases working for big, important corporations. Every summer there was a party, and the firm chartered a yacht.

I had struggled for so long. I had scrimped on food and worn my socks until my toes popped out. I couldn't imagine having so much money. But I knew I would like it! I would like working in a beautiful office with assistants and secretaries. All that money and power could assist me later on to help my people. That was the way my friend Tomás looked at it. He had accepted such a job.

Then I visited the firm in the barrio. One of the partners, Angelique Lopez, waved me in and invited me to join her and the others in a celebration. They had won a case for an undocumented worker who had been injured on the job. The radio was playing, and everyone was holding a paper cup of wine. One of the legal secretaries danced with a lawyer. Everyone was laughing. Angelique warned me not to think that every day was like this. "Usually, it's doom and gloom around here," she said. But I looked around and knew it wasn't true.

That night I sat with my father on folding chairs on the sidewalk. I thought of how I missed the barrio during my schooling. I had missed the colors

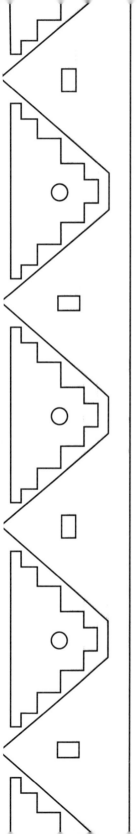

of the women's dresses, the smells of spicy beef in the *tacquerias*, the sounds of salsa music. There were bad things in this neighborhood, too, of course. Gangs, drugs, hopelessness, injustice.

What was the best way to fight that injustice? To make money, to be powerful? Or to work, day after day, on little cases to help one person at a time? That night, I wasn't sure—I'm still not sure. All I knew that night was that I'd liked Angelique and her laugh, and the secretaries, and the cake, and the client who had toasted them with tears in his eyes. I had felt at home there. I took the job.

There are many ways to help my people. This is my way.

* * *

━≡ 5 ≡━

Life-styles

———

Culture

Not all Mexican Americans have the same life-styles, but when so many live in communities together, their customs and habits tend to be similar. Though some are rich and some are poor, Mexican Americans share many beliefs and experiences.

There more than 12 million Mexican Americans in the United States today, and they are estimated to be the second-largest non-Anglo group in American, outnumbered only by African Americans. Currently Mexican Americans rank fifth in national ancestry groups in the United States, following English, Germans, Irish, and Italians. Their number exceeds that of French, Polish, and Scottish Americans.

More than one million Mexican Americans arrived legally between 1980 and 1989; it is virtually impossible to measure how many came illegally, but it could be as high as six million. Mexican Americans make up almost two thirds of the total Hispanic population of this country and have a culture different from other Hispanic groups such as Puerto Ricans, Cubans, Dominicans, and South Americans. Most live in the states on the border of Mexico, such as Texas, Arizona, New Mexico, and California, but many have recently settled in Washington, Oregon, Michigan, Illinois, and other states where jobs can be found. In each of these states one can find areas where Mexican culture lives on.

As mentioned in chapter 1, much of the Mexican culture in this country today was introduced when Mexican territory became

A makeshift home in northern San Diego County. Poverty is rampant in many parts of the barrio.

U.S. soil. Those first Mexican Americans had no desire to change their culture overnight to fit their new citizenship. Instead they nurtured their Mexican roots and created the distinctly Mexican flavor found in much of the American Southwest. This flavor is perpetuated by the new Mexican immigrants arriving each year.

Many Mexican Americans find comfort in the barrios, which are essentially clusters of "Mexicanness." For new immigrant families, the barrios are a place where they can adapt to their new surroundings at their own pace. Many Mexicans do not speak English before coming to the United States, so areas where Spanish is spoken freely make a new Mexican American feel less helpless.

Many Mexicans also come to the United States knowing little about American customs. The barrios provide a place where new arrivals can overcome their shyness about being in the United States. People who have lived there longer act as teachers, showing how to get along as a Mexican here. In the barrios, Mexican Americans also learn that their traditions need not be abandoned, because the combination of Mexican and American ideas has become a culture of its own. Many Mexican-American cultural groups, following the example set by the Chicano movement, are discovering and promoting this unique Mexican-American society.

Yet the barrios can also be limiting, for many of their inhabitants fail to learn English well or to adjust to the customs of their new country. While keeping the Mexican culture alive is very important for Mexican Americans, it can also hurt them by alienating them from American society. They may have a harder time finding jobs because their English is limited. Their children may need special attention in school because English is not spoken at home. Not knowing American customs can hold them back from participating in American society and can open them up to hurtful ridicule from the people around them. Mexican Americans living in the barrios usually have to work harder than other Americans to achieve the same goals in school and in the workplace.

The economic situation of the barrios also limits many of their residents. Though the word barrio literally means "neighborhood," it has come for many to mean "ghetto," because poverty often thrives there. When a Mexican American does not have the money to continue with school or even with English lessons, he or she has less of a chance of getting out of the ghetto. Because Mexicans are usually poor when they leave Mexico they arrive in the barrios with little or no money; whatever money they do have buys even less in the United States than it did in Mexico. And because Mexicans come to the United States in large numbers, one family moving out of the barrio is usually replaced by several more moving in. Life in these neighborhoods can be defeating and depressing, especially when it appears as if the dire situation can never change. Perpetuation of poverty and separation from American culture are continued generation after generation in an unending cycle.

Yet living in culturally separate neighborhoods like the barrios is not unusual for new immigrants. Italians, Poles, Jews, Chinese, Germans, and others who immigrated in large numbers at the turn of the century or earlier often lived in isolated areas where most of the residents spoke their native language. Some of these areas still survive: "Chinatown," "Little Italy," and "Germantown" are still used to describe parts of some large American cities. For Mexicans the period of heavy immigration has not yet ended, so these "Little Mexicos" will continue to exist in many urban areas for generations to come.

Education

In 1982 the Supreme Court ruled that undocumented immigrants have the same right to a free education as any American citizen; this was a great victory for Mexican Americans especially. *Plyler v. Doe* was argued by MALDEF (the Mexican American Legal Defense and Education Fund) on behalf of 15 children of undocumented immigrants who could not pay the tuition that local Texas school boards were asking them to pay. In some places this tuition was as high as $1,200 a year. MALDEF filed the action on behalf of the undocumented immigrants so that they would not have to be exposed and subject to deportation; they were identified only as "John Doe" or "Jane Doe."

The state of Texas argued that the presence of these students would place a "significant burden" on the state's finances and that the availability of free public education would encourage illegal immigration. The Supreme Court ruled that the undocumented workers were protected by the Fourteenth Amendment, which says that "no state shall . . . deny any person within its jurisdiction the equal protection of the laws." The Court felt that the undocumented immigrants were entitled to the same rights as anyone else in the United States, including the benefit of a free education, and that the states could not create laws that inhibited them from enjoying this right. They also noted that the state of Texas had not proven its view that a ruling in favor of MALDEF's clients would harm the quality of education in Texas. In his opinion Justice

William Brennan wrote, "By denying these children a basic education, we deny them the ability to live within the structures of our civic institutions, and foreclose any realistic possibility that they will contribute in even the smallest way to the progress of our nation." Justice Brennan argued that by denying these children an education, they will only continue to be a burden on the state.

Schools are supported financially by a combination of property taxes and funds that come from state taxes and lotteries. Though undocumented workers pay taxes (directly through withholding on their paychecks and indirectly through the part of their rent that goes toward property taxes), they pay much less in taxes than it costs to educate their children in school. For Mexican-American families, this discrepancy is even larger, as their families tend to have more children than Anglo-American families. The more children in school, the more money it costs to support

Mexican-American high-school students. In 1982 children of undocumented workers won the right to attend public schools with their American counterparts.

their education. States that have a high population of undocumented immigrants are particularly hard-hit when trying to fund
education for children whose parents' low incomes do not greatly
support the state budget. Local governments argue that the federal government should pay these children's tuition, insisting that
lack of federal supervision of the border lets in the illegal workers
in the first place.

As Justice Brennan noted, there are benefits to providing
these children with an education. Since many undocumented
immigrants are permanent residents of the United States, their
children will grow up to be an integral part of American society.
The more education they receive, the less they will be dependent
upon the government and others to make a living and the more
they will be able to contribute to society. A country never loses
when its residents get an education.

Even after the Supreme Court ruling, however, Mexican-
American children do not seem to be getting an education equal to
their Anglo counterparts. Forty percent of Chicano students drop
out of school before they finish high school (as opposed to 13 percent of Anglos). In addition, only 7 percent complete four years of
college. Many immigrants, including Mexican Americans, consider getting an education and learning English to be a major advantage for their children, but the children may be inhibited by the
parents' own lack of education. Children need many things to get
a good education, including proper nutrition and help with home-
work. Many Mexican-American families may have difficulty meet-
ing these needs.

Even if these children did have more schooling it would be no
guarantee of success. Each year of education beyond high school

does not earn a Mexican American as much money in the workplace as it would an Anglo, possibly because of prejudice and discrimination. Yet Mexican Americans who go to college have hopes for their careers and for their futures that are no different than the aspirations of Anglos, African Americans, or the members of any other group.

Unfortunately, Mexican Americans seem to have the country's next-to-lowest educational achievement, second only to Native Americans. Though Mexican Americans are better educated than they were a few years ago, their average level of education is not rising as fast as it is for other immigrants or for native-born Americans. Poverty and language barriers surely contribute to this low standing, but one of the greatest handicaps could be the way Mexican-American children think of themselves based on what our culture tells them. Prejudice against Mexicans has not disappeared; children may hear the false beliefs some bigoted Anglos harbor about Chicanos, including that they are naturally lazy and stupid. Any child told that he or she is inferior may believe it and may live up—or down—to that image in school.

Currently a great argument is raging over whether to educate Mexican Americans in two languages—in other words, to give them a bilingual education. Many schools in Mexican-American communities in the border states have set up programs in which children spend much of the day speaking Spanish. This process helps many Mexican immigrant children to overcome the difficulties of their first year in a new country when they are still uncomfortable with English, a time when they might be unfairly labeled as slow learners. Lessons are taught at the same pace as those in English-only schools, but both English and Spanish are used to teach them.

The people who want bilingual educations for their children feel that it is their right. However, many schools argue that bilingual education costs more than they can afford, since special teachers and books must be used. Other critics of the bilingual approach say that children who are unable to learn in both English and Spanish will be thought "slow," that their comprehension of English may be delayed because they are encouraged to rely on their Spanish. Many native-born Americans oppose bilingual education altogether, insisting that as immigrants *choose* to come to this country, they should accept the conditions and the language they find here.

Mexican-American children in an elementary school. The pictures on the board show the influence of bilingual education.

(continued on page 87)

Luis Salazar
The First Day of School

Luis Salazar's parents came to the United States illegally when he was 2 years old. He is now 19, a high-school dropout who is studying for his high-school equivalency exam. He works as a waiter in Tucson, Arizona.

My very first day at an American school was pretty bad, and it went downhill from there. I was six and I thought it was the greatest thing that ever happened to me, to be going to an American school. I had been looking forward to it all summer. My older brother Arturo took me. He held my hand and kept telling me to slow down. He was in no hurry.

The big brick building was ominous. The thing that worried me most was the *Ingles*, the English. I only knew a few words. Neither my mother nor my father spoke English. My brothers and sisters knew a little, at least, but Arturo and my sisters Maria and Lourdes spoke too fast for me to follow.

Arturo told me to be good as he showed me my classroom. I walked in with my brand-new schoolbag. I took a seat way in back. There was a book on the desk with a shiny new cover. I was afraid to touch it, in case it belonged to someone else. The cover was bright blue, and it had a picture of a blond girl and boy on it. It was the most beautiful book I'd ever seen.

I felt shy. The children were all strangers. It took me a few minutes to realize that I did recognize three of my classmates. Mario, Roberto, and Alma all lived near me. They looked strange in their dress-up clothes and carefully brushed hair.

The teacher came in. She was Anglo, but she looked nice. I sat up straight, my hands folded, the way my mother had told me to sit. The teacher began to read the names of the students. The names all sounded foreign to me, and I guess I started to daydream. Then the classroom fell silent. The teacher was looking over her paper at the class.

"Lou-ees?" she said.

My hand shot up. "Here," I said. Arturo had told me to say "here" when my name was called.

Suddenly, the whole class burst out laughing. It was like a wave hitting me in the face. I realized that they were laughing at me. I felt my ears burn and my face get hot. Had I said the wrong word?

The teacher smiled. "Lou-eeeze," she said. "I'm looking for Louise Campbell."

Mario was two seats in front of me, and he turned around and mouthed, "A girl," in Spanish. He looked sorry for me. It was the first day of school, and already I had made a terrible mistake.

I hung my head. The class was still laughing, and the teacher said something sharp to them. She was probably telling them to be quiet, but I didn't know. My ears were buzzing, and I couldn't understand a word.

The boy behind me kicked my chair. "Louise, Louise," he said in a low voice so that the teacher couldn't hear. "Why do you have a girl's name, Louise?"

The boy on the other side of me laughed behind his hand. "Why didn't you wear your dress today, Louise?"

I caught the word *dress*. I knew that word. My hands were wet, and I

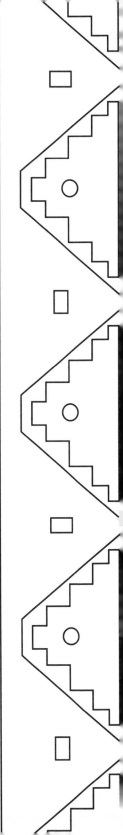

rubbed them on my new pants, the pants my mother had bought for me for my very first day of school. They were way too long in the legs, so she had pinned them up, talking to me while she worked about how many friends I would make and what a smart boy I was. She told me that I needed to smile and look people in the eye, like a confident American boy. She told me to be kind and friendly.

"Hey, Louise," the boy behind me said. He said something in English that I didn't understand. But I knew it wasn't something friendly or kind. I guess I started to cry, and that made it worse. The boy across the aisle laughed and I heard the words *girl* and *dress*. I opened the book on my desk. It was full of words I didn't understand.

After that, nobody made friends with me except for Mario and Roberto. We spoke Spanish all the time, so my English didn't get much better. I knew that my mother didn't understand why I hated school. She would shake her head and wonder what had happened to her smart boy Luis. Not Lou-eeze. Luis. I knew what had happened. They had taken my name from me. They had made me ashamed of my very own name.

Nevertheless, more and more schools are starting programs in bilingual education, and more and more schools are finding that Hispanic children learn as well as any others. Though many Mexican-American parents are slow to learn English, mostly because they don't have the time to participate in activities that use English or do not have the educational opportunity to learn it, their children in bilingual education programs work hard and are successful at learning English.

Working Conditions

Mexican Americans hold many different kinds of jobs. Some are doctors, lawyers, or shop owners; some are managers, supervisors, factory workers, or farmhands. A majority of Mexican immigrants come to the United States for job opportunities in manufacturing and farming. Most of them are undocumented.

Because not enough employers pay Mexican Americans as well as they pay Anglos, Mexican Americans bring in on average just under three quarters of what Anglos make. Many Mexican Americans live below the poverty level, earning less than the government thinks they need to live comfortably. A larger percentage of Mexicans than Anglos live at this low-income level. The lower average age of Mexican immigrants compared to other immigrants and to native-born Americans may explain why Mexican Americans as a group are paid less. Younger Mexican Americans are certainly not going to make as much as older workers of any group.

Usually the employers who pay Chicanos less have been hiring them for years. Employers who hire Mexican Americans for the first time are likely to pay them at the same levels they pay their other employees. This is very promising news for Mexican Americans breaking into occupations where other Hispanics have not worked a lot—as professionals or business executives.

Manuel Cuevas, clothing designer, displaying fashions that evoke traditional Mexican design. Mexican Americans who own businesses can provide equal pay and fair treatment to Mexican workers.

Mexican Americans are now also managers in many of the
industries where they have labored for so long. Factory and farm
owners are learning that Mexican Americans in positions of
authority make their relationships with their workers much better,
and that Spanish-speaking supervisors who understand the customs of the workers tend to make better managers. Over the last
10 to 15 years Mexican Americans have been placed in more and
more important work positions.

More Mexican-American women are going to work than
native-born American women, since so many need to participate
in the support of their families. These Mexican-American women
are paid closer to what Anglo women are paid, unlike the greater
difference in wages between Mexican-American men and Anglo
men. Unfortunately, this is likely because Anglo women already
make substantially less than Anglo men.

For undocumented immigrants who work as unskilled factory
workers or farmhands, the chance of being treated poorly by
employers is great. Many employers take advantage of these
workers, who are afraid to report bad working conditions because
they fear being deported. In 1979 a Louisiana chicken farmer was
arrested and later convicted of chaining two undocumented workers around the neck and turning them into slaves. In other areas
where undocumented immigrants work there have been reports of
50 people quartered by their employers in two rooms, of laborers
watched over by armed guards, and of workers being shipped
around the country in trucks.

Not all undocumented workers live under such conditions,
however. Some make good money in blue-collar jobs in the cities,
as factory or construction workers, and often join or run labor

unions. Many fill positions in the hotel and restaurant business or work as domestics. Yet many continue to be treated poorly by employers because they do not know their rights. They do not collect workers' compensation when they get hurt; they do not have medical benefits when they get sick. Unions are working to teach these laborers that they have the right to be treated as fairly as any American citizen, as guaranteed by the Fourteenth Amendment.

Hiring undocumented immigrants has been illegal in this country since 1986, which makes it difficult for many newly arrived Mexicans to find jobs at all, and which may contribute to the fear and abuse they endure when they *can* find work.

Religion

Most Mexican Americans look to their families and their religion as the foundation on which their lives are built. Most Mexican Americans are Roman Catholics because the Spanish who conquered the Native Americans in Mexico were ardent Catholics. In fact, Hispanics are the largest group of Catholics worldwide, and the largest group of ethnic Catholics in the United States, having come to outnumber Italian-American Catholics. Yet many Mexican Americans are turning away from Catholicism and becoming Protestants, in a quest for a church that better meets their needs.

Catholicism in Mexico did not start with a single priest or minister. In 1531, reports of a vision of the Virgin Mary, known subsequently as Our Lady of Guadalupe, converted many Mexicans of Native-American origin to Catholicism. The Mexican Catholics practiced their religion with fervor.

Preparation for a first communion in the Catholic church. Religion plays a major role in the lives of many Mexican Americans.

As Spanish missionaries left Mexico, particularly when some of Mexico became United States territory, Mexicans started practicing their religion at home. Most of the American Catholic churches were run by French and Irish Catholics, and Mexicans felt uncomfortable among English-speaking priests with American customs. On both sides of the border they took their religion out of the church and into the home. Much of this popular religion, or religion of the people, has been carried by Mexican immigrants to the United States. Many Mexican-American homes have an *altarcito,* a little altar, where devout Catholics pray each day.

Committed Mexican-American Catholics do, however, go to church more often than native-born American Catholics, often praying at the church during the week as well as on Sunday. For many Mexican Americans, though, the church cannot offer them the sense of community and comfort it offered them in Mexico. In rural areas of Mexico the local priest is not only a clergyman, but a counselor, a doctor, and an arbitrator. American priests do not take on those roles, and many of them do not speak Spanish, even in areas with many Hispanics.

Recently, many Mexican-American and other Hispanic Catholics have turned to Protestant churches where the ministers are more willing to speak Spanish. The churches, less strict than Catholic churches, also accept Mexican-American customs developed in home-church practices. Many Mexican Americans also cite the excellent Bible studies offered by the Protestant churches as a reason for their attendance. They claim that the Protestant churches know more about the Bible than the Catholics do, and that they want their children to get this knowledge. Still, when it comes to sacraments such as marriage, baptism, Communion, and last rites, Mexican Americans are likely go to a Catholic church to receive them.

Unfortunately for the Catholic church, there are fewer Mexican-American Catholics in recent years than in the past. The fewer there are, the fewer may become priests and nuns who might balance out the lopsided hierarchies of the churches that lack Chicano clergy. The Protestant churches, especially the

Baptists, seem to be gaining at the expense of the Catholics. As of 1980, Texan Baptist churches had more than two million Hispanic members. The Mexican Baptist Bible Institute had 100 Hispanics studying to be ministers while a nearby Catholic seminary had only 30 candidates for the priesthood. Mexican Americans are also becoming Mormons, Jehovah's Witnesses, Episcopalians, and Lutherans, and are joining many other Protestant religions.

In an effort to influence the American Catholic church to meet the needs of Mexican Americans, the Mexican American Cultural Center and a group called Los PADRES have dedicated themselves to teaching Anglo priests about the history of Mexicans and the church. These organizations are trying to pave the way for new churches in Mexican-American areas that can offer the linguistic and cultural understanding and sympathy their potential parishioners may already see in Protestant churches. These groups also push for the ordination of Mexican-American priests and bishops and teach Spanish language ministry. Catholicism is rooted so deeply in Mexican culture that if the American Catholic church makes a concerted attempt to reach out to Mexican-American Catholics, it will surely lessen the trend toward Protestantism.

Racism

Because Mexican Americans are such a large and visible minority in the United States, there are bound to be clashes based on prejudice and mistrust between Chicanos and other ethnic or racial groups. In areas where many different cultures meet, the presence of Mexican Americans has often led to hostility and violence.

In Los Angeles and other cities with youth gangs, race plays an important role in gang warfare. Not only are there Chicano gangs, but there are Anglo, African American, Filipino, Chinese, Vietnamese, and other ethnically derived gangs. Sometimes the feuds between these gangs are based solely on ethnic differences. In parts of the country where gangs are not as prevalent, racial differences can still prompt hate groups such as the skinheads or the Ku Klux Klan. Mexican Americans have often been the target of these groups.

Clashes develop when two groups do not understand or

Graffiti showing Chicano pride. Viva la Raza means "long live the race," a reference to Chicanos.

accept the differences between their cultures. Mexican Americans, who pride themselves on preserving their heritage, are often targeted in hate crimes. They may also strike back against their tormentors or commit violence against other ethnic groups, especially in areas where Mexicans are the majority. Mainly because they refuse to assimilate into American culture or deny their Mexican background, Mexican Americans have been targeted by groups hoping to eliminate all cultural diversity in America.

Racism takes on subtler forms, as well. Often residents of an Anglo neighborhood may keep Mexican Americans from moving into the area by simply refusing to sell them a house. No matter the status, poor or rich, of a Mexican-American family, many Anglos consider Hispanics to be "undesirable" neighbors. Anglo politicians may see to it that voting-district lines are drawn so that Mexican Americans never get a political majority in one area, and they may exploit fears Anglos have of Mexican Americans to gain votes in an election. By constantly pointing out differences, real or false, between themselves and Mexican Americans or other ethnic groups, prejudiced people can perpetuate false stereotypes and alienate minorities even more.

Mexican-American Art

Mexican-American art has thrived since the 1800s, but the most prominent artists have emerged in the 20th century. Trained artists, mostly muralists, left Mexico as refugees of the 1910 Mexican Revolution and brought their art to America, where their work was avidly commissioned. Seasoned muralists, such as Diego Rivera and David Alfaro Siqueiros, brought the Mexican

(continued on page 99)

—≡ 95 ≡—

Richard Peña
Call Me Doctor Peña

Richard Peña is a doctor in a large midwestern city. He was born in Los Angeles, California, and is a third-generation American.

I guess I was always aware of prejudice, but I didn't think about it too much. From the time I entered grade school to the day I finished college I had Anglo friends who treated me as an equal. When I went to medical school I thought being a doctor would guarantee me respect. But one day last summer I met a man who made me realize that the title of "Doctor" doesn't guarantee a brown-skinned man anything at all.

I wasn't exactly lost that day, but I didn't really know where I was, either. I was on my way to buy some medical textbooks that I'd seen advertised in the paper. A doctor was moving and she was selling her textbooks, cheap. So I looked at the map and figured out which bus I needed to take to the suburbs. Unfortunately, I miscalculated and got off the bus too early. I would have to walk another 15 blocks to reach the address listed in the ad.

It took me only two blocks to see that the residents of this town weren't used to people of color. I was the only dark-skinned person on the street, and people were either staring at me or, it seemed, trying not to.

It was a hot day. There was no shade on the main street, and the side-walks bounced the heat back up in my face. I decided to get a cold soda and drink it while I walked.

When I pushed open the door of the store, the man behind the counter looked at me hard. It was a look I recognized right away. What are you doing here? the man's gaze said. I am keeping an eye on you.

I decided not to let it bother me. I got a cold can of soda and waited behind a woman customer at the counter who was paying for her purchases. She handed over a bill, and the counterman made change. The woman thanked him and turned. When she saw me she almost jumped back. Then she quickly switched her purse to her other shoulder and inched past me.

I smiled politely at the counterman, but he didn't smile back. Instead his eyes slid away from me and he looked at a woman who was browsing through a rack of paperback books. "Can I help you?" he asked the woman.

"Just looking," she said.

I put the can on the counter. The counterman pretended not to see it. "Excuse me," I said, and took out my wallet, waiting for him to tell me how much it was. But the counterman ignored me as he snapped open a newspaper and scanned the headline. I started to get angry, but I told myself not to make a scene, to just buy the soda and leave.

The woman chose a book and walked over. She waited politely behind me, but the counterman held out his hand for the book. "I'll take that," he said.

She looked at me, then back at the counterman. "But—"

"I'll take that," the counterman said.

Slowly, she handed him the book. I saw that her neck had turned red. She was embarrassed. But not embarrassed enough to say, "No. This man was first."

Rage swept over me. I glared at the counterman, who stared back as he handed the woman her change. I wanted to grab his collar and shout at him, but instead I took a five-dollar bill out of my wallet and put it on the counter. Of

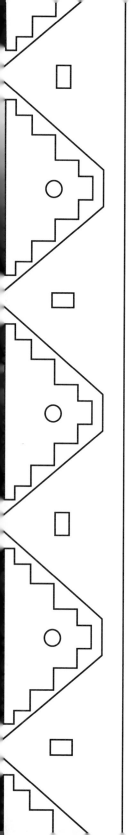

course it was way too much money, but there would be no question that I'd left enough. I walked toward the door with my soda.

The counterman called out, "Don't you want your change, *Pedro*?"

I turned. "My name is Richard," I said quietly. "But you can call me Dr. Peña." My voice had no trace of an accent. I saw that the man was surprised. He probably thought that I was a farm worker.

And if I had been? I wondered. Suddenly I was angry at myself for telling the man that I was a doctor. Every man is entitled to respect. A medical degree shouldn't make a difference when a man is thirsty and needs a drink.

I pushed open the door, and for a moment the sunlight was blinding. Everything looked too bright: The sky, the sidewalks, even the grass seemed bleached of color. When I closed my eyes, all I could see was white.

I tossed the soda into a trash can. I knew that I would be thirsty on my long walk, but I didn't care. I *wanted* to be thirsty. It would help me remember.

✳   ✳   ✳

Mural Renaissance of the 1920s to the United States of the 1930s.
Siqueiros was commissioned to paint murals in Los Angeles's
Plaza Art Center and the Chournaid School of Art, while Rivera's
works graced San Francisco's Golden Gate Exposition and New
York's Rockefeller Center (whose owners had the mural destroyed
because it contained a portrait of the Russian Communist Lenin;
Rivera, however, reproduced the mural). Other Mexican emi-
grants, such as José Clemente Orozco and Rufino Tamayo, whose
murals appear in New York's New School for Social Research,
Dartmouth College in New Hampshire, and Smith College in
Massachusetts, learned their trade in the United States rather
than in Mexico.

From the 1930s through the 1960s Mexican-American muralists thrived, and artists in other media also strongly explored their
Mexican heritage. Octavio Medellín's sculptures, Chelo González's
colored-ink drawings, Antonio Garcia's murals, and Rubén
González's collages reflected the confusion these artists felt about
being both Mexican and American. Though they proudly celebrat-
ed a Mexican heritage dating back to the Aztecs and Mayans and
extending to modern Mexican villages and people, these artists
felt like outsiders from the art world because they were Mexican
American; their sense of alienation, of not belonging, influenced
their work.

With the rise of the Chicano movement in the 1960s, art was
perceived by many Mexican Americans to be a means for political
or cultural statement. "Chicano Art" became a medium through
which Mexican Americans could deal with and express the political and cultural confusion they faced. Influenced at first by the
black civil-rights movement, and later by the Vietnam protestors,

A Mexican-
American mural in
East Los Angeles.
The mural has
become a strong
medium for
Mexican-American
artists.

the Chicano Moratorium, *La Crusada para Justice,* and the farm
workers' movement, Hispanic artists created posters and murals
that made strong political statements about the problems
Mexicans faced in the United States and about possible solutions
to those problems. Murals painted during the 1960s and 1970s

showed Chicanos active in their communities, while posters of the 1970s and 1980s pointed out the harsh realities faced by farm workers or undocumented immigrants. Ester Hernandez's *Sun Mad* (1982) parodied a famous raisin-box design, with a skeleton dressed as the Sun Maid maiden and the caption "Unnaturally grown with insecticides, miticides, herbicides, fungicides" (Mexican Americans picking grapes for raisin companies were supposedly exposed to these chemicals). *Undocumented* (1981) by Malaquias Montoya showed a silhouette of a figure, meant to be an undocumented immigrant crossing the border, caught on the barbed-wire fence.

Modern Mexican-American art continues to follow the tradition of the "Chicano Art" movement. It reflects how the cultures of the two countries blend into each other in some ways, yet remain distinctly separate in others. Unfortunately, Mexican-American art has not been recognized nearly enough by the American art world, mainly because it has often been considered unsophisticated.

Mexican-American Literature

Since the Chicano movement, Mexican-American literature has tackled many of the same themes as Chicano art. Beginning with José Antonio Villarreal's 1959 novel *Pocho*, Chicano literature has dealt with the conflict many Mexican Americans feel between their Mexican and American lives, mixing historical fact with a mysticism typical of Latin-American fiction, a mysticism often condemned by critics as being a way to deny the realities of the Mexican-American situation. Zeta Brown, the protagonist of Oscar Zeta Acosta's two novels, *Autobiography of a Brown Buffalo* (1972) and *The Revolt of the Cockroach People* (1974), struggles with living during the heart of the Chicano movement in an Anglo culture while coming from a Mexican heritage. Acosta even has his hero meet and talk with Cesar Chavez. Yet Ron Arias's *The*

Road to Tamazunchale (1975) is set purely in the imagination and memory of the main character. And *The Plum Plum Pickers* (1969) by Raymond Barrio and *". . . and the earth did not part"* (1971) by Tomás Rivera both portray the very real struggle of Mexican-American farm workers.

Themes of land and family are strong in Chicano literature, surely because these are strong themes in Chicano life. And Mexican Americans' real-life struggle for political, economic, and cultural strength are often supported in literature by a celebratory attitude toward life.

The Blend of Mexican and American Cultures in the United States

At the same time that Mexican-American culture has been the target of criticism, it has also found its way deep into the American life-style. As much as Mexican Americans are influenced by their new culture in the United States, Americans have been influenced by the culture of Mexico. Beginning with the first Mexican Americans, Mexican immigrants have brought with them wonderful arrays of traditions, foods, design, and language that have been incorporated into American life, sometimes so much so that Americans may not realize their Mexican origin.

Mexican design has become an integral part of American culture. Pottery, architecture, weaving, and interior decoration copying Mexican American styles are popular throughout the country, especially in the Southwest. Houses designed like the Spanish-style houses in Mexico are common in the border states, especially in the areas where 16th- and 17th-century Spanish missions and churches already give the land a distinctly Mexican flavor. Rugs, blankets, and vases made using Mexican techniques are also found in American homes throughout the country.

Mexican food has become extremely popular in America in the last few decades. Tortillas, burritos, tacos, margaritas, nachos, quesadillas, and guacamole are all recognizable foods in any part of the United States. Most of this food, however, is modeled after a cuisine called *Tex-Mex*, named after the combination of cooking styles found in Texas and Mexico—truly a blend of the two cultures. Yet traditional Mexican food is also popular in the United States. Mexican restaurants can be found all over the country, even in places where no Mexicans live. New York City, which has only a few Mexican-American residents, has hundreds of Mexican restaurants. The United States even has Mexican fast food, perhaps the most American of cuisines!

Most American children can tell you what a piñata is, and how you play with it. On their 15th birthdays many Mexican-American girls celebrate with a quinceañera, including a mass and a big party—almost like a wedding! And many Americans join in the Cinco de Mayo (Fifth of May) celebration, a holiday commemorating Mexican victory over French invaders in 1862.

Perhaps the greatest indication of Mexican influence on American culture is in language. So many Spanish words have made their way into American English because of the Mexican American culture that thrives in the Southwest. Words like *siesta, bonanza, fiesta, rodeo, mesa, canyon,* and *coyote* are all familiar to Americans and appear in American dictionaries. In addition, many

Mexican influence has made its way into American life, from pottery to rugs to foods like hot peppers, tortillas, and beans.

place-names in the Southwest are Spanish in origin: Los Angeles, San Antonio, El Paso, San Diego, California, and Colorado are all either Spanish or Spanish-derived.

All of this simply highlights how closely aligned the cultures and peoples of Mexico and the United States already are. With the help of education, training, and fair treatment, Americans of Mexican origin will realize the dreams they hoped for while living in the small towns of Mexico. Mexicans will continue to come to the United States, and the people who already live here, who owe much of their history and civilization to their southern neighbors, must make more room for this growing minority. They must teach Mexicans, but they must also learn from them, because Mexican Americans bring so much with them to their adopted country.

For Further Reading

Acosta, Oscar Zeta. *Autobiography of a Brown Buffalo.* San Francisco: Straight Arrow Books, 1972.

———. *The Revolt of the Cockroach People.* New York: Bantam Books, 1974.

Anaya, Rudolfo A. *Bless Me, Ultima.* Berkeley, Cal.: Quinto Sol, 1972.

Arias, Ron. *The Road to Tamazunchale.* Reno, Nev.: West Coast Poetry Review, 1975.

Barrio, Raymond. *The Plum Plum Pickers.* New York: Harper and Row, 1969.

Catalano, Julie. *The Mexican Americans.* New York: Chelsea House, 1988.

Chicano Art: Resistance and Affirmation, 1961-1985. Los Angeles: Wight Art Gallery, University of California at Los Angeles, 1991.

Davis, Marilyn P. *Mexican Voices—American Dreams: An Oral History of Mexican Immigration to the United States.* New York: Henry Holt, 1990.

Dunnahoo, Terry. *Who Cares About Espie Sanchez?* New York: E.P. Dutton, 1975.

Gomez, David F. *Somos Chicanos: Strangers in Our Own Land.* Boston: Beacon Press, 1973.

Halsell, Grace. *The Illegals.* New York: Stein and Day, 1978.

Kessner, Thomas, and Betty Boyd Caroli. *Today's Immigrants, Their Stories.* New York: Oxford University Press, 1982.

Levy, Jacques E. *Cesar Chavez: Autobiography of La Causa.* New York: W. W. Norton, 1975.

Light, Ken. *To the Promised Land.* New York: Aperture, 1988.

———. *With These Hands.* New York: Pilgrim Press, 1986.

Moore, Joan W. *Mexican Americans.* Englewood Cliffs, N.J.: Prentice-Hall, 1976.

Quirarte, Jacinto. *Mexican American Artists.* Austin, Tex.: University of Texas Press, 1973.

Rivera, Tomás. *". . . and the earth did not part."* Berkeley, Cal.: Quinto Sol, 1971.

Rodríguez, Armando Rafael, ed. *The Gypsy Wagon.* Los Angeles: Aztlán Publications, 1974.

Rodriguez, Richard. *Hunger of Memory.* Boston: D. R. Godine, 1982.

Samora, Julian, and Patricia Vandel Simon. *A History of the Mexican American People.* Notre Dame, Ind.: University of Notre Dame Press, 1977.

Young, Jan. *The Migrant Workers and Cesar Chavez.* New York: J. Messner, 1974.

Index